MIGRATION CAN FALL APART

Life Stories from Voluntary and Deportee Return Migrants

O. Alexander Miller

University Press of America,® Inc.
Lanham · Boulder · New York · Toronto · Plymouth, UK

Copyright © 2008 by
University Press of America®, Inc.
4501 Forbes Boulevard
Suite 200
Lanham, Maryland 20706
UPA Acquisitions Department (301) 459-3366

Estover Road
Plymouth PL6 7PY
United Kingdom

British Library Cataloging in Publication Information Available

Library of Congress Control Number: 2007942928
ISBN-13: 978-0-7618-4000-8 (paperback :   )
ISBN-10: 0-7618-4000-1 (paperback :   )

For Mama—Edna,

Wife—Paulette

and

Children—Paige and Zachary.

CONTENTS

FOREWORD

Alex Miller's book can be read and appreciated on a number of very different levels.

As a scholarly work, there is his hypothesis of "colonial capital" which he artfully employs to shed light on, and explain, the starkly different experiences of the (trans)migrants in his sample.

But what I found even more fascinating and touching, on a personal level, were the stories told, and the insights offered, by the (trans) migrants themselves. Not so much for their truth value or explanatory power, but for the windows they opened into the lives of these people caught up in, and swept along by, international forces and systems beyond their control and comprehension.

In fact, although Dr. Miller amply illustrates his arguments and cases with extensive and well-selected quotes from his in-depth interviews, I found myself wanting to know even more about these people, their experiences and how they struggled to make sense of them.

I thought others would too, and so I urged him to publish his study in a forum that would make it available not just to academics, but to a wider audience who would enjoy spending time with, and learning from, these very engaging people.

I am pleased he has done so.

Enjoy.

Patrick D. Nolan
University of South Carolina

PREFACE

Migration phenomena have been written about in many ways, but the significance of immigrants' pre-migration experiences and how they affect migration and return migration outcomes have not been well researched. This should not be the case, as analysis of pre-migration experiences is central to constructing adequate theoretical statements about migrants who share a common ethnicity, but have different migration and return migration experiences. To illustrate the effects of pre-migration experiences I introduce the concept of "colonial capital" and use it as a predictor of migrants' experiences abroad, and on returning to home societies. "Colonial capital" derives from a quartet of deeply held prejudices about: (a) family and skin pigmentation, (b) education, (c) social graces, and (d) financial capital. The mere acquisition or possession of any one element is of little utility in achieving the immigrant dream of higher socio-economic status. In Jamaica the exhibition of prejudice can take many forms such as thinking kindly about another person but acting negatively towards them; thinking negatively about another person but acting positively toward them, or both thinking and acting negatively towards another person (Merton 1989). However, it is a sign of good social graces to think negatively about others but act warmly toward them. This cultural practice lies at the base of Jamaican relationships and between returnees and countrymen.

The elements in colonial capital serve two purposes—migrants use them to make sense of their foreign environs, and others use these elements to judge each migrant. As a Jamaican immigrant to the U.S., I experienced some of this. In 1986 I was awarded a scholarship based on my educational achievement. However, a few days after arriving in America, I drew upon my formative experiences by asking for, "the telephone book." Having come from a society where a home telephone was a luxury and the telephone book for the entire island was a fraction of an inch—I asked a librarian at Erskine College, in Due West, South Carolina, for the American telephone book. He responded, "which one?," while pointing to the shelf of thick telephone books for different cities. Although I was accepted by the school for my education, other elements in my colonial capital did not sit well with the community at large. Hence, on the first day I was warned that, as a black person, I should not to be caught in a bar after dark. After twenty years of living in the U.S., the reverse now occurs, on trips to Jamaica I am judged by my family of origin, educational achievement, financial capital and social graces. I am still seen as the not-so-dark skinned child of a primary school teacher and a landlord who has improved the educational element of his colonial capital, but one who has also declined by adopting American ways.

Since researchers have not paid attention to the significance of colonial capital, they have overlooked the various categories of migrants within ethnic groups, and misjudged the adequacy of their theoretical explanations. This is the utility of the concept of colonial capital—it provides a parsimonious multivariate prism to identify hitherto missed categories of migrants, and specifies the sole category to which the theory of the day, Transnational Theory, applies.

A cursory reading of the literature over the past ten years, or so, leaves one with the impression that transnationalism is a given for all migrants. But as my research indicates, Transnational Theory does not apply to all groups of migrants. There are at least three types of migrants, and transnationalism applies only to those with mid-colonial capital. My position is supported in this book by the life stories from immigrants, and through an examination of how low-, mid- and high-colonial capital affect migrants' quest for social mobility in host and home societies.

This book represents my contribution to migration theory by proposing a theoretical model which considers forced return immigrants, commonly called "deportees." Currently all of the theories: Neo-classical Economics (NCE); New Economics of Labor Migration (NELM); Structuralism and Transnational Theory apply only to voluntary migration. Hence, there is need for new theories to apply when immigrants are deported and prohibited by force of law from carrying out the presumed cycle of arrival and departure in similar fashion to voluntary return migrants. In my research, this emerging feature of deportees in return migration is addressed theoretically by clarifying the claims in Transnational Theory and using colonial capital at the time of migration as the predictor of migrants' lives abroad and on returning home—even if they return 30 to 40 years later.

This new theory that I propose is called Colonial Capital Theory of Migration (CTM). My central argument is that, "migration and return migration experiences are as complex and varied as one might expect, given migrants' pre-migration colonial capital, and associated shifts in cultural values and economic mobility in host societies." Migration absolutely falls apart for migrants who have extremely low-colonial capital—at the time of migration and return migration they have little education, family support, financial resources and social graces. Abroad they are vulnerable to sharp declines in identity and socio-economic mobility, which are exacerbated by being deported to home societies where countrymen hold ancient prejudices about socio-economic mobility—deportees cannot overcome prejudices as they lack the resources to complete rites of return passage such as building large homes. In the case of migrants with mid-colonial capital, they acquire wealth abroad, but improving this one element does not protect them from migration and return migration disappointments, and challenges to their self-identity—faced with this predicament, mid-colonial capital migrants try to find solace by constantly engaging in transnationalism. Unfortunately, circuitous international travel, and transfer of ideas between home country and host country is not salutary. In each country migration can fall apart as mid-colonial capital migrants constantly face unwanted prejudices about other colonial capital elements of skin tone, poor education, and social graces. High-colonial capital migrants stand in stark contrast to all other migrants, as they have the necessary family support, enough formal education and social graces to successfully negotiate their way in host and home societies without engaging in constant transnationalism.

Although the data came from just one West Indian island, Jamaica, it is my hope that the concept of colonial capital will find utility in the study of other immigrants.

A number of persons have been influential in the development of my ideas and my awareness about migration issues. Included are: Dr. Jimy Sanders, Graduate Director in the Department of Sociology at the University of South Carolina, who introduced me to the seminal works of Vickerman (1999) and Waters (1999); Dr. Patrick Nolan, who is the past Department Chairman, and current Professor of Sociology at the University of South Carolina. He found the life stories compelling and suggested that I should publish my work. Dr. Kwame Dawes, Director of University of South Carolina Arts Institute. He supported my academic growth and helped me to sort through the details of publishing. Dr. Paul Higgins, Sociology Professor at the University of South Carolina, who taught me about field research.

I thank: Dr. Bernard Headley, Sociology Professor at the University of the West Indies, for his review of the final manuscript; Mr. Hugh Miller, Mr. Percival LaTouche, Miss Adlyn Wilson, Dr. Elaine Campbell, Mr. and Mrs. Wilbert Sirjue, Mr. Errol Reid, Mr. Trevor Nation, Mrs. Barbara Nation, Mr. Duhaney of the Montego Bay Poor Relief for their support in gathering data; and the many return migrants who took the time to grant me unpaid in depth interviews—especially Victor, Hugh, Cleveland and Reg.

CHAPTER ONE
Introduction

Rationale for Research
Migration Can Fall Apart brings together compelling life stories about Jamaican return migrants—some were deported and others returned voluntarily after having migrated to the United Kingdom (U.K.) in the 1950s, or the United States (U.S.) after the passage of the 1965 Immigration Act. The sheer numbers of voluntary return migrants are impressive (see Table 1.1 below) and the social issues revolving around them are significant.

Table 1.1: Number of Returning Residents to Jamaica, 1993-97

Year	UK	US	Canada	Other	Total
1993	919	988	278	178	2,363
1994	1,145	999	333	110	2,587
1995	1,007	905	288	153	2,353
1996	995	863	296	114	2,268
1997	995	762	244	91	2,092
Total	5,061	4,517	1,439	646	11,663

Source: Returning Residents Facilitations Unit, Ministry of Foreign Affairs and Foreign Trade, Jamaica Customs and Excise.

Unfortunately, migration movements can produce fractured familial bonds (Bodnar 1985, Mahler 1995), and end in forced return migration. In Jamaican the population of deported migrants mirrors that of voluntary return migrants (see Table 1.2 below)—Jamaica is one of the top ten countries for deportations from the U.K. and the U.S.

Table 1.2: Immigration to Jamaica, 1997-2002

Year	Voluntary Returnees	Deportees
1997	2,092	1,699
1998	1,875	2,161
1999	1,765	2,071
2000	1,282	1,730
2001	1,177	2,529
2002	1,113	2,003

Source: Ministry of National Security and Justice
Ministry of Foreign Affairs and Foreign Trade.

The existing migration research literature offers valuable guidance about the race based experiences that Jamaicans have abroad. In the U.S. and U.K. they experience cross currents which stem from being socialized in West Indian societies where race is downplayed, but migrate to societies where race is used as the major organizing principle (Vickerman 1999). In the U.K., their reception is especially harsh. Absent a highly integrated West Indian community to fulfill their needs for cultural expression, and facing extremely limited economic opportunity, Jamaicans along with other West Indians confront the full brunt of racial discrimination. In the U.S., first generation Jamaican migrants tend to experience initial success because of their good work ethic. Eventually, however, they are identified (along with native born blacks) by race as inferior and this decouples them from optimal success (Waters 1999). Due to the decline in industrial jobs, the concentration of Jamaican households in inner cities, and negative race labeling, subsequent generations have few opportunities. Eventually Jamaican migrants (1st and 1.5 generations—those children who were born in Jamaica but later joined their parents abroad) can become discouraged and consider their options for returning home. In response to the cultural realities of structural racism, Jamaican migrants tend to strengthen their transnational ties with their home island and make preparations for returning by sending remittances (Thomas-Hope 1986, 1988, 1999).

Although some attention has been paid to West Indian return migration (Brookes 1969; Brooks 1975; Davison 1968; Hinds 1966; Gmelch 1980; Noguera 1999; Goulbourne 1999), the lion's share of current research is on post-1965 immigrants in America (e.g., Waters 1999, Vickerman 1999), the effects their remittances have on West Indian economies (Thomas-Hope 1988, 1986, 2001), and the personal freedoms female migrants gain abroad (Pessar 1997).

To help overcome past omissions, this book takes a fresh approach to explaining migration experiences. It uses the pre-migration lives of migrants as a predictor of their migration and return migration experiences. Although voluntary return migrants to Jamaica tend to have adequate financial capital to negotiate re-entry into local communities, and enter social structures which they already know, studies show that they face unexpected challenges related to the sense of their own identities as true Jamaicans versus how they are identified by countrymen—as oddities (Goulbourne 1999).

This research also sheds light on the cadence of vulnerability, the shame in deportee return migration, and the backlash effects that this category of migrant has on Jamaican society and institutions. The central theme in migration is achievement of social mobility (Bennett 2002), hence deportation is a major unanticipated eventuality which negates the achievement of this end. The negative impact of deportation is seen in newspaper reports describing some deportee return migrants as homeless, hapless and hopeless; having to live in shelters and on the street (*Jamaica Gleaner,* October 2003).

In some ways the homelessness of deportees is similar to being homeless anywhere. Their financial capital does not afford them the opportunity to purchase shelter, and they are impaired in ways which negate being able to maintain independent living. Research about return migration shows that as return migrants negotiate re-entry into Jamaican communities, the building of luxury houses is an integral rite of passage. The life stories about deportees show how involuntary return migrants who are stigmatized and have little or no financial capital to participate in transnationalism, adapt to, and negotiate re-entry into Jamaican society.

The overall study contributes to existing research literature by assessing how the paths which involuntary and voluntary return migrants take to achieving adaptation converge and diverge due to their colonial capital at the time of migration. Analysis is explored through a transnational theoretical perspective because it represents the way current scholars see Jamaicans, as persons who conduct their lives across national borders. Furthermore, Transnational Theory is useful in explaining the interlocutor between pre-migration experiences, the transnational identity which mid-colonial capital migrants develop abroad from the effects of racism, and how they subsequently perceive their situation among countrymen—who are also engaged in transnational activities.

Salient Features in Jamaican Society which Encourages Migration

I now introduce the reader to salient features in Jamaica's history which spawns international migrants whose relatively low colonial capital decouples them from success.

The island of Jamaica, my home country, lies 90 miles (150 kilometers) south of Cuba and 100 miles (160 kilometers) west of Haiti, its two nearest neighboring countries. The latitude and longitude of the capital, Kingston, are about 18 degrees North and 78 degrees West.

Though the island was discovered for Spain by Christopher Columbus in 1494, its major formative culture is British, as in 1655 the Spanish were evicted by the British. During the colonial era, from 1655 to emancipation in 1832, indentured laborers of Jewish and European ancestry were brought to West Indian colonies to produce tobacco for the economic expanse of the British Empire. Eventually colonists saw greater profit in growing sugar, but the indenture system failed to provide the necessary labor. As a solution, colonists turned to African slave labor, but once slavery became unpopular the British colonists emancipated their slaves. To fill the labor shortage indentured laborers were brought again, but this time from India and China. Eventually, these racial groups intermarried to produce Jamaican society from a varying mixture of Europeans, Jews, Africans, Indians, and Chinese races.

At the top of this stratification system were English people, followed by mulattos, Jews, Chinese, Indians, and blacks (Phillips and Phillips 1998:16). In the British West Indies, English colonial values still shape social and institutional life, even though over time various other Caribbean ethnic groups have gained access to the top of the stratification hierarchy and the significance of race is now well hidden behind education and social class (Kuper 1976; Stone 1991).

Colonialism affected Jamaica negatively by creating a weak economic structure which forced labor to migrate in order to achieve economic stability (Thomas 1973; Glass 1960; Davison 1962). Since profits from exported sugar and tobacco were used to boost the British economy, but not that of Jamaica, when slavery ended in 1838, Jamaicans were left with inadequate manufacturing infrastructures to sustain their booming population. Additionally, Colonialism nearly stripped the African population of its culture by setting in place an English framework for achieving success and respectability through European religious and educational institutions.

Some researchers argue that there was a positive side to colonialism, though not often mentioned, Caribbean people acquired globalized world views (Phillips and Philips 1998:17). This vista helped them to appreciate that their national identities were shaped by the caprices of other societies; especially Britain (Nettleford 1968). To support this positive view of their heritage, some Jamaicans even claimed that they knew more about Britain than about Jamaica (Phillips et al. 1998).

Despite this one positive, colonialism has had a net negative effect on the Caribbean. Once British presence was removed from colonies, Jamaicans, like other West Indians migrated locally, regionally, and then to England so as to relocate the British colonial resources which became invaluable to their sense of identity and social status. After the end of slavery, ex-slaves took to foraging for work within the confines of their islands, and eventually to wherever labor was needed, such as in Panama, as well as other West Indian islands. Between 1832 and 1850 internal migration occurred as emancipated slaves moved from plantation to free holdings (Gmelch 1992), and moved to rented land or took over abandoned estates. During this period labor became short in some islands such as Cuba, and thus existing laborers from other Caribbean islands, including Jamaica, migrated to Cuba for the purpose of growing sugar cane.

Between 1850 and 1920 the migration of former slaves and their immediate descendants followed foreign investment into other regions. For example, between 1904 and 1914 migrants went to help build the Panama Canal. But the available work was not enough to absorb a growing Jamaican labor pool. After the 1920's a period of economic decline set in and this slowed migration. The economic slump was broken by World War II which instigated a new wave of Jamaican migration to Britain, the United States and Canada, as labor was needed to help in the war effort, and migrants desperately wanted to achieve a standard of living to satiate their foreign consumption habits (Foner 1983:9). The scale of this wave of migration has been dubbed "mass migration." Over a ten year period West Indian islands lost up to 5% of their adult population and Jamaican migrants accounted for 25% of the total numbers who migrated from the Caribbean region (Chamberlin 1997; Gmelch 1992).

A small portion of Jamaican mass migrants to Britain eventually furthered their education. Numbered in that population of first generation migrants to Britain were people who have since gained prominence in Caribbean politics and entertainment, such as: Dudley Thompson; Forbes Burnham; and Lord Kitchner. But, a survey of West Indians showed that one out of four was a non-manual laborer in their home country (Gmelch 1992), and over time the proportion of unskilled laborers increased in the migration stream. Not only did the level of skill change as mass migration proceeded, but the age and sex of Jamaican migrants changed from being predominantly adult males, to being females and dependents under age 18. Gmelch (1992) argues that from 1952 to 1957, seven out ten migrants were male, but after the Commonwealth Immigration Act in 1962 which restricted black migration to Britain, the stream became predominantly female and children under 18. The males and females who went to work, and some say to help in the World War II effort began to settle in areas of Britain that could not attract white laborers, who now moved to more attractive Regions of London and Yorkshire. This is important to note so as to highlight that although there was a labor shortage across all occupational categories, mid-colonial blacks were permitted to only fill those jobs that whites left. In fact, Britain did not intend to hire any West Indians because they were seen as a disruptive presence and as people who were failures; even before they migrated to compete for opportunities in the United Kingdom (Harris 1987).

Theoretically, Jamaican mass migration has been explained by economic and demographic changes in Jamaica (push factors). The combination of rapid West Indian population growth, without commensurate economic growth, has sustained a structural need for West Indian migration. Take for example, the city of Kingston, Jamaica, which was founded in 1692 as a commercial center. In 1943, despite migration to Central America and the United States, the population grew from 27,400 in 1861 to 237,000. By 1960 it is estimated that 10,000 people entered the labor market every year, but the economy lacked the capacity to absorb them in manufacturing or service industries. Idle boys and men were supported by their mother, aunts, or grannies who worked as domestic servants. Explanations have also considered economic developments in foreign countries (pull forces) (Foner 1978; Chamberlin 1997; Bennett 2002).

Critics of the Push-Pull theory of migration argue that there is a tendency to not acknowledge the political and historical structures which link host and sending societies, and the structural conditions which impel the decision to migrate. In their analysis Marxist theorists, dependency theorists (Watson 1982) and world system theorists (Wallerstein 1974) argue that international migration is one outcome from structures of dependency and the transformation of labor power into a commodity which flows from periphery to core societies such that the necessary labor for capitalist accumulation is mobilized externally through the creation of labor shortages in one place, and the over supply of labor in another. After World War II, capital was removed from the Caribbean where there was an over abundance of labor and invested in Britain where there was shortage of labor (Harris 1987; Watson 1982). This meant that labor had to move to Britain also.

Where females were concerned, migration gave them social freedoms and occupational opportunities hitherto denied in Jamaica, for girls tended to be sheltered by their guardians and confined to the perimeter of their homes. Also, females tended to earn less than men, and this made women dependent on their spouses. In 1983, sixty four percent of West Indian women in London claimed that they were more independent than in Jamaica. The majority attributed this independence to greater employment opportunities, higher wages than in Jamaica, less scrutiny from the community than in Jamaica, and the opportunity to achieve new work skills (Foner 1983).

Such a glib description of female independence defies reality. West Indian women had to match their domestic responsibilities with working. Also, women were not only doing double duty at home and work, but were paid as part time employees while working full time hours (Lewis 1993). Female clamor for social and perceived economic independence, created backlash, as voids were created which remained unfilled, and female migrants in foreign counties experienced much inequality in opportunity (Bennett 2002). Women left behind children, and parents to be cared for by relatives and by others in a society where there were few elderly care facilities. From 1955 to 1960 Jamaican adults migrated with only 65,000 children while leaving 90,000 behind to be cared for by relatives (Gmelch 1992). Although the opportunity to work represented an improvement in income over Jamaica and women gained financial independence, yet Jamaicans declined socially because they were always seen as black, of the lower class, and inferior. From the beginning Jamaicans, like other West Indians, filled the dirtiest and worst paid jobs. Foner (1978) states:

> Still, like their male counterparts, upwardly mobile women are ambivalent about their life in England torn many times between improvements in their occupational status, income and living standards, on the one hand, and the decline in their status as blacks, on the other (Foner 1978:115).

By and large, West Indian migrants were unprepared for the very poor reception and treatment they received in Britain. Whites displayed open anger and youths armed with a variety of weapons attacked blacks in their homes and in one instance a young carpenter was murdered while walking home (Gmelch 1992). Women who were recruited as nurses experienced inequality by being tracked into the least prestigious areas of nursing such as midwifery and ancillary staff. Women trained as nurses in the Caribbean did not receive the promised work permits, which led to unemployment in the Caribbean (Bennett 2002). While British society looked down on Jamaicans because of their race, Jamaicans looked down on British society for the uncleanliness of its people.

But, this treatment did not deter Jamaican migrants because they knew that British society was not a melting pot in which West Indians could achieve structural assimilation. Furthermore, they could not become English for that was reserved for whites who were born in England (Phillips and Phillips 1998). The demeaning level at which West Indian blacks would be accepted by the English was determined at least three centuries previously when Africans slaves produced wealth for the British Empire, and each time that European masters and mistresses copulated with Africans who they saw as property. In a sense West Indian migrants presented themselves in British society as an indefatigable consequence of colonialism, and this was not debatable. Whether or not West Indians were liked or hated by British society, they felt as if they had a right to be in England, having come from authentic British colonies.

When the infamous Immigration Act of 1962 was crafted to stem the tide of West Indian migration, a backlash occurred, and many West Indians who would have left Britain remained there, and many in the West Indies who would have waited until jobs were available in Britain decided to migrate before the window of opportunity closed. Hence, more Jamaicans and other West Indians flooded Britain than had been planned for or expected, and British anti-immigration sentiments grew.

The eventual precipitous increase in West Indian migration to America is attributable to the British Government curtailing the entry of West Indians with the 1962 Act, and America opening her doors to them through the passing of the 1965 Hart-Cellar Immigration Reform Act which permitted West Indian migration to America due to family reunification. Previously, only 3,000 migrants were allowed in based on race, now 120,000 were permitted from the Western Hemisphere. Between 1965 and 1968, 140,827 West Indians migrated to the United States, of which Jamaicans accounted for the majority (Kessner et al. 1982).

The Hart-Cellar Immigration Act gave rise to a distinct female pattern of migration which was different from that of the British in which males dominated. The migratory process could take up to ten years to reunite a family. This practice still exists today and produces fractured families and "left behind" relatives. (Foner 1983; Crawford-Brown et al. 2001). Here again as in Britain, Jamaican migrants' economic pursuits superseded their ethnic identity and familial bonds. The law permitted domestic workers, and nurses, hence nearly 50% of legal professional Jamaican immigrants were female and nurses (Foner 1983). The entry of large numbers of professionals also gave rise to a distinctive core of workers which was different form the British migration of mainly blue collar workers.

Returning Home
It is a sociological axiom that every migration stream generates a counter stream (Koch 1977; Newton 1984; Richardson 1983). Some researchers argue that this statement is clearly truer about Jamaican migrants (Thomas-Hope 1985; Davison 1968) who went to Britain, than those who went to America. Jamaicans, these scholars argue, who went to England planned to stay for only five years and then return to Jamaica. Although history shows they had to stay for 30 to 40 years to become financially stable, their commitment to returning remained firm. In 1983, fifty percent of mass migrants interviewed planned to return to Jamaica indefinitely within the next ten years, and 43% would return if

they won the lottery. In contrast, in America 33% said they planned to return and only 8% if they won the lottery (Foner 1983). The differences have been attributed to the acuteness of the climate and racial experience in Britain, and also to the fairly easy access to America resulting from the geographical propinquity of America to Jamaica. Jamaican migrants in America can travel back to Jamaica more frequently and move to the warm climate of Florida which mimics that of Jamaica (Foner 1983:34). But, as shown in Table 1.1 current return migration from both countries approximate each other.

But, returning home can fall apart in various ways. Just as migrants experienced fractured families by leaving behind parents and children in Jamaica to negotiate their way among people and land they did not know, on returning they now leave behind children and those with whom they created strong bonds, to negotiate their way back into Jamaican society, a land they call home but a people they no longer know.

Migration can also fall apart for migrants who are eventually deported, as they are not only denied re-entry into host societies but into home communities. West Indian deportation is a new phenomenon, and an emerging sociological issue about which little academic work has been conducted. Reports show that Jamaicans form the largest single group of inmates in British prisons, having been convicted of crimes such as drug trafficking, and murder (*Jamaica Gleaner*, 2004). America and Canada have adopted the same approach as Britain: to send foreign nationals to their home countries to reduce crowded prisons and the cost of running them—once in Jamaica, deportees are considered free.

The impact of deportees on Jamaican society appears to be severe, as the Jamaican police and public blame them for the sharp increase in murders and gang activity (*Jamaica Gleaner*, June 11, 2004). To stem the negative impact, voluntary return migrants have suggested that deportees should be taught a skill before being released, but the problem is also with the Jamaican economy which is unable to provide enough employment for the existing population, much less for additional groups.

Since the 1950s, not much has changed about the imbalance between employment opportunities and population growth in Jamaica (Clarke 1983). According to statistics from the Economic and Social Survey, in 2003, there were over 141,000 unemployed persons consisting of 58,000 males and 83,000 females (*Jamaica Gleaner*, August 8, 2003). This number represents an unemployment rate of 12.8%, and of the total number of unemployed persons, 84,000 are in the 20 to 35 age group.

The above *Jamaica Gleaner* report also cited a number of important comments about the social ramifications of high unemployment. For Karl Samuda, general secretary of the Jamaica Labor Party (one of Jamaica's two major political parties), unemployment is the most difficult problem facing the young in inner-city areas. For Noel Cowell, lecturer in the Department of Management Studies at the University of the West Indies, Mona, unemployment is a major problem that breeds fathers who are failing to maintain their children because they cannot stand up to their economic responsibilities. The newspaper report also cited Barry Chevannes, a Sociologist at the University of The West Indies, who argues that unemployment is a serious problem especially because of its chronic nature. In the last two decades there have not been enough jobs to absorb people coming into the labor market.

For Father Houlong, a Catholic Priest and organizer of food shelters, after 42 years of independence there is a greater disparity between the few rich and the massive number of poor in Jamaica. Jamaica suffers from larger numbers of totally marginalized people than ever before. Jamaica has more homeless and destitute people than any other island in the English speaking Caribbean—out of a national population of approximately 3 million, in Kingston, Jamaica's capital, there are approximately 500,000 poor or marginalized people (*Jamaica Gleaner*, August 9, 2004).

Jamaican towns are riddled with: poverty; unemployment; inadequate housing; poor educational facilities; and jobs are becoming increasingly menial— sometimes requiring a first degree from a recognized institution. The case of Gazelle captures the severity of poverty in Jamaica. After graduating from the Engineering Department at the University of Technology, she was contacted by a company in Kingston for an interview. However, she made an enquiry on the telephone about the vacant position before the date of the interview. They were seeking college graduates to work as telemarketers for JA$100 (approximately US$1.40) an hour (*Jamaica Gleaner*, August 9, 2004). In a second case, a student who graduated from the University of the West Indies was offered a tour guide's job that was provided through the University's job placement program.

In sum, return migration is taking place in an impoverished economy and these fuels the prejudices of countrymen and the disappointing experiences of mid-colonial capital return migrants.

Theoretical Rationale

Besides Transnational Theory, there are at least three other major theoretical explanations for return migration. These are Neo-classical Economics (NCE), New Economics of Labor Migration (NELM), and Structuralism (Cassarino 2004)—but all have weaker explanatory powers than Transnational Theory, and more critically no current migration theory applies to deported return migrants.

The NCE perspective argues that migration is a rational decision in which wage differentials, availability of employment and the cost-benefits to migration are calculated. Labor migration occurs when the differences in wages or employment opportunities abroad are large enough to encourage investing in the initial costs of migration in anticipation of higher earnings which may accrue over time (Todaro 1969). The incentives to migrate are greater in communities where current wages are low and the prospects for income growth are poor, than in communities with high wages and job prospects (Harris and Todaro 1970; DaVanzo 1981; Mincer 1987). Return migration in this perspective results from failure to achieve the anticipated job and higher wages in host societies.

Neoclassical models of migration have been central to most explanations of Jamaican migration. Jamaican migrants are in search of greater employment opportunities and higher wages. This model also dominated the literature about the expected effects of the North American Free Trade Agreement (NAFTA) on migration from Mexico to the United States. Over a short term, migration from Mexico to the United States was expected to increase as trade barriers were removed. However, in the long term, migration to the United States was expected to decline as foreign companies invested in backward communities and as the wage gap between home and host societies shrank (Cornelius and Martin 1993).

In contrast to NEC, the New Economics of Labor Migration (NELM) argues that laborers migrate to acquire capital which is remitted to home societies for investment in entrepreneurial activities, building homes, or purchasing major durable goods. Migration and remittances play an important role in agricultural modernization and the development of a small business sector in rural villages and towns (Stark 1991; Taylor 1999). Once the household in the home society achieves their set economic goals return migration occurs.

Both the NEC and NELM perspectives argue that migration is a calculated plan in which migrants expect to achieve set economic goals. However, both approaches have weaknesses which derive from their univariate explanation of return migration as due to economic factors. As such return migrants and their experiences are analyzed only in economic terms, and leave unexplained the identities of returnees, their personal experiences abroad, and how they are received in their home communities. In any approach to analyzing Jamaican return migration these are important issues. Also though return residents to Jamaica amass large sums of money, yet other issues are operative, such as the fact that the cost of living in Jamaica has risen sharply, and returnees experience jealousy from their compatriots (Goulbourne 1999; Davison 1962).

Also, left unexplained are salient features in West Indian return migration. In the first place the observed tendency in West Indian return migration is for under and over achievers of estimated economic goals to not return. Economic under-achievers such as retirees cannot risk reverting to their former economic level (Taylor 1976). The over-achievers may return if they can be guaranteed a comparable life style to the one they achieved abroad. One of the reasons for returning is the discontentment migrants feel with their lives abroad and their feelings of inferiority (Davison 1962). A second factor is the cluster of personal crisis such as divorce, death of a spouse or trouble with health or their children. Older immigrants complain about loss of health from exposure to severe cold weather (Taylor 1976). A third factor is attachment to the land of their birth, which for some scholars is the main reason West Indians give for return migration (Gmelch 1992).

In contrast to the above two theoretical perspectives, the structuralist approach draws its analysis of migration from systemic factors and structures of production. Structuralists focus on three systemic processes that drive migration: uneven penetration of capitalism in home and host societies; commodification of production which in turn undermines subsistence production in home societies; and the proletarianization of labor. The demand condition (push factors) for migration is driven by the relatively low penetration of capitalism, oversupply of cheap labor, and the undermining of subsistence production in home societies.

The supply trajectory (pull factors) of this process, however, is shaped by a constellation of interests of the ruling states inclusive of a relatively high penetration of capitalism, and need for cheap labor.

The decision to return involves the migrant's expectations, and favorable economic, political and social conditions within the home country. An example of a structuralist study is Cerase's (1974) which argues that the type of return migration is linked to the stage in the process of acculturation that migrants reach in America at the time of their return. In this regard Cerase identified four main types of returnees:

(a) "Return of failure" refers to migrants who could not become integrated in host societies due to prejudices, and returned to their home societies. Having been away for a brief period 0 to 5 years, return of failures reintegrate into their home society as if they never left.

(b) The "return of conservative" group overcome culture shock in host societies and begins to identify with the new society even to the point of linguistic acculturation. These migrants return in 5 to 10 years after completing predetermined goals in the home country such as buying land and building new houses.

(c) The "return of innovation" group represents migrants who endure past their target date for return and stay long enough, 10 to 20 years, to experience social mobility's glass ceiling. These migrants reach an advanced stage of acculturation and take back innovative ideas to their home societies for personal use and to help their relatives. They do not plan to change their home society but help to preserve its traditions.

(d) The "return of retiree" group represents those migrants who reach retirement, but respond to the call of nostalgia to live peacefully in their home country. They have stayed away for so long, 20 or more years that their political or economic viability is minimal. Also, their retirement may just suffice because over time housing and cost of living have escalated exponentially.

King (1983) argues, if the time abroad is too short, then the migrant will not have acquired enough human and financial capital to effect change back home, and if they have been away for too long then they stand the chance of being alienated from the structure of power relations and may be too old when they return.

The "return of innovation" group is made up of those migrants who went abroad to amass capital and achieve skills for realizing their goals at home. However, on actually returning home their objective is impeded by structural forces which maintain traditional power structures. Simply being abroad may not mean one has acquired the necessary information and economic power to enact change, as there are structural forces of which the migrant is unaware. Return migrants are perceived by structuralists as being ill-prepared for returning, as not only skills and financial capital are necessary. While away changes in home societies occur necessitating a period of readjustment to structural realties within local communities (Gmelch 1980).

In the structuralist view, the locality of return is important as the expectations of returnees are shaped by family and friends back home. In a study about return migration to Nevis, one interviewee said, "If I didn't have anything I would never go home. You look like a fool to go with nothing." (Olwig 1993:183) In order to be accepted, return migrants conform to the conspicuous habits and expectations of their stay-at-home family and the local community at large. Often, resources acquired abroad are invested in taking care of stay-at-home family members, building luxury homes and buying cars rather than in agricultural machinery (Byron and Condon 1996). Large luxury homes provide clear evidence that migrants have achieved socio-economic mobility.

While the structuralist view is useful in highlighting that return migration is not only shaped by the experiences in host societies, but also by power relations back home (Lewis and Williams 1986), it is criticized for two reasons, first for assuming that migrants live in host societies which are disconnected from home societies and always have too little information with which to make informed decisions (Murphy 2002), and second, for employing a bimodal theoretical framework which falsely portrays migrants as permanent fixtures in either host countries or home countries. Also, this bimodal framework focuses on the movement of people but fails to explore how capital, ideas, and a wide variety of goods are continuously moved by migrants across national borders.

A growing body of literature argues that migration movements are not static, many individuals, and not just the merely lucky, determined and gifted can move from one country to another with little impunity (Zelinsky 1971:224), and are better described as transnational. This term captures the continuous striving for *socio-economic mobility* through the perceptible movement of people, ideas, and various forms of capital across international borders, and the *bifocal identity* which is formed as a result of exposure to home and host societies. The concept of transnationalism, entered the field through the work of an anthropologist, Szanton-Blanc to describe the social connections between countries.

Over the last ten years scholars have increasingly argued that international migration is a complex process in which migrants no longer feel attached to any one country and so hold multiple identities, frequently move capital, ideas and variety of goods between home and host societies—Transnational Theory is an attempt to create a conceptual framework for these ongoing activities (Cassarino 2004), and transmigrants are the persons who forge and maintain transnational links (GlickSchiller et al. 1992). From a transnational perspective then, contemporary West Indian migrants and especially females, build and maintain links between themselves to form a community of transmigrants, while maintaining links between home and host countries (Pessar 1997).

Despite the utility of Transnational Theory, it fails to identify the various categories of migrants within ethnic groups, those who are truly transmigrants, and totally disregards the emergence of deportees. There is therefore need for a new theory, which I argue can be constructed by using the concept of low-, mid- and high-colonial capital as a predictor of migration outcomes. Through this parsimonious multivariate prism, precise analysis of migrants' experiences can be performed. This is clearly illustrated in subsequent chapters, by showing that Transnational Theory applies only to mid-colonial capital migrants. In home and host societies, often their migration movements not only produce economic success but fractured ethnic, familial and community bonds (Bodnar 1985; Mahler

1995; Wierzbicki 2004), and the reconstructed identities represent unwanted continuities or roles that migrants thought had been left behind. In the case of low-colonial capital migrants, they suffer rejection, but do not have the means or freedom to be transnational. High-colonial capital migrants' education, social graces and family support enable them to settle happily in home societies.

The new theory being proposed—Colonial Capital Theory of Migration (CTM) states that, migration and return migration experiences are as complex and varied as one might expect, given migrants' pre-migration colonial capital, and associated shifts in cultural values and economic mobility experienced in host societies. Colonial capital is case sensitive and is derived by understanding the historic prejudices which determine the social life of different ethnic groups. In the case of Jamaican migrants to the U.S. and the U.K. these elements are (a) family and skin pigmentation, (b) education, (c) social graces, and (d) financial capital. The mere acquisition of any one element is of little utility in achieving higher class status. Scholars debate the significance of race and education (Kuper 1976; Stone 1991; Vickerman 1999) in a changing Jamaica, but none would question that these are master variables which determine Jamaican experiences at home and abroad. A review of Jamaica's history and current discourse substantiates the significance of these elements. From the time of colonialism up to the 1970s, social classes tended toward homogeneity in high-colonial capital. For example, light skinned Jamaicans were the most educated, had more financial resources, and held coveted occupational opportunities in every commercial activity. But, in the 1970s a concatenation of forces contributed to the economic and educational mobility of lower class Jamaicans. For example, the rise of the People's National Party (PNP) and Prime Minister Michael Manley to political power blackened the nation through free education which increased the occupational opportunities of lower class dark skinned Jamaicans in institutions.

In response to the unraveling colonial system of prejudices, wealthy high-colonial capital Jamaicans kept control of their Jamaican assets, but moved abroad. This ushered in a period of upward mobility for low-colonial capital Jamaicans who filled their void. Concomitantly, Reggae music (Jamaica's national music form) and Rastafarianism (a religion of the oppressed) gained enough prominence that social heterogeneity was bred among people in different social classes as they shared a common music, dress, and language. Also, disheartened low-colonial capital migrants, living abroad, now saw Jamaica as a place of promise and made remittances in preparation for returning, and to help relatives make use of unprecedented opportunities. As a result, the standard of living increased, and poor low-colonial capital countrymen built homes and bought modern automobiles with their newly acquired income. These improvements in colonial education and financial capital were seen in the "blackening of the Jamaican nation," or the occupational and political rise of lower class dark skinned Jamaicans and their unprecedented acquisition of status markers through transnational trade (Robotham 1998, 2000).

During the 1980s, when the Jamaica Labor Party (JLP) came into power, the programs which were instituted by Michael Manley were reversed. But, since then, the blackening of Jamaica has resurfaced in the public's rejection of

Edward Seaga; a former JLP prime minister who is light skinned, and the 17 year tenure of Prime Minister Hon. P. J Patterson, who is popularly acclaimed to be the first black skinned prime minister. As a consequence of the 1970s groundwork, and PNP Prime Minister Patterson's regime, well educated dark skinned Jamaican entrepreneurs from the lower class have constructed unprecedented transnational business ties spanning major cities in America, Canada, England, Japan, Thailand, Malaysia and Africa. Streets are now lined with: "deportees" a label Jamaicans apply to pre-owned imported Japanese automobiles; American farm produce; and merchandize previously found only in city stores owned by light brown skinned Jamaicans.

But, despite these shifts, by and large, Jamaica exhibits deep inequality and prejudices between groups with different skin shades. At one extreme, the lighter skinned Jamaicans control the wealth and tourism; which is the major foreign currency earner in the economy. At the other extreme, although the darker skinned low-colonial capital Jamaicans have small shops, transnational connections and mobility through education and politics, yet they suffer from high unemployment rates, and are perceived to be wanting in one or more elements of colonial capital. To address their predicament, and heighten their status, some dark skinned women have resorted to bleaching their skin. Brown women are still considered to be more beautiful, and dark-skinned women tended to see light-skinned males as a pathway to improving their stock and the life chances of their children.

It is to this society that between 1993 and 1997, twenty-one thousand mid-colonial capital migrants returned (see Table 1.1), to find an ancient colonial system of prejudices in which returnees' pursuit of wealth abroad, without commensurate changes in other colonial capital elements, did not improve their return migration experiences. In the eyes of some returnees, blackening of the Jamaican political system was commensal—without improvements in social graces. In other words, the low–colonial capital of politicians and the Jamaican populace was at the heart of returnees' poor reception.

Data Collection

Data to illustrate the effects of colonial capital were collected in the form of life stories from a non-random snowball sample of twenty-eight Jamaican return migrants over the course of three years in Jamaica, West Indies. In addition to attending various functions with return migrants, a total of twelve weeks was spent conducting face to face interviews with 17 voluntary return migrants, of which in depth interviews were conducted with six male and six female return migrants who were willing to tell their stories in detail. Eleven deportees were also interviewed. Some follow-up interviews were done by via e-mail and telephone conversations. Where possible, interviewee's stories were triangulated for veracity, with their children, friends and relatives. Migrants' "colonial capital" at the time of leaving Jamaica was used as the predictor of migration and return migration experiences. Colonial capital derives from a quartet of ancient prejudices about: (a) family and skin pigmentation, (b) education, (c) social graces, and (d) financial capital. The mere acquisition of any one element is of little utility in achieving higher class status.

Collecting life stories provided return migrants with an opportunity to retell their stories in ways which reached beyond what is currently presented in published documents, and connect the past to the present through the process of reflection—while understanding their everyday lives. Some scholars see life stories as too particular to explain social concepts (Somers and Gibson 1994:39), but others argue that social action can only be understood when we recognize that people act according to the relationships in which they are embedded—these are captured in life stories (Somers 1994:67).

In life stories people freely manipulate, and transform cultural plots to suit their needs, therefore how they construct themselves changes according to the cultural plot being utilized. I was keenly aware of these elements in the stories being told that return migrants as actors were constantly embedded in one culture or another culture. When migrants told their life stories, they used culture plots to create their personal stories about how they made sense of their lives amidst prevailing ideologies. I emulated Douglas (1976) by allowing return residents to determine what was important to talk about as topics came up. In this approach interviewees raised issues not contained in the original question guide (Denzin 1978). Though I permitted free conversation, I ensured that pertinent questions were covered by creating a basic question guide which captured my understanding of the experiences of migrants. When conversation lapsed, this list of questions came in handy to spur the interview along.

As Frank (1979) argues, life stories are the product of the interviewer and interviewee, and therefore it is essential for the interviewer to tell their story. Liebow (1993) encourages the researcher to divulge something about their background as it bears on the work at hand, for the information is filtered through the idiosyncrasies of the researcher and reflects their bias and social position. However, the claims of collaboration between interviewer and interviewee can be overstated, some aspects of a researcher's interpretation may change with another interviewer, but validity and reliability demands that the essential characteristics in a researcher's analysis should remain the same. Gmelch (1992) uses Freeman's (1979) analogy of a photographer who shapes the images by controlling the lighting and by cropping. Some features of the subject will be emphasized by the photographer, but none would mistake the subject's likeness for someone else—even if it is a caricature.

I was born in Spaldings—a town that is located in the center of Jamaica. My mother was primary school teacher, and father owned houses and worked in several accounting jobs. I went to my mother's school from age 1 through age 12 and then to Knox High School. During the 1960s life appeared to be good as the Jamaican dollar was on par with the US dollar, and agricultural produce was king in the local economy. Jamaica had just gained independence in 1962 and each year there were many joyous celebrations on Independence Day—August 6th. There were many other national holidays, but the most memorable was Christmas time when the local dentist dressed up as Santa Claus and drove through town throwing gifts from the back of his Land Rover van. In addition, he sponsored merry-go-round rides and festivities on his large estate. As I think about this dentist he was light skinned. Back then life was organized communally, and people shared in each others life. For example, a parent would call a Police Inspector to scold a child, if one was ill they could see the pharmacist who would suggest a remedy. If an adult saw a misbehaving child they could reprimand them without any retribution. However, eventually this changed starting in the 1970s.

Having both grown up in Jamaica, and lived abroad, I resonated with the stories returned migrants told. I know the Jamaican society that mass migrants expect to find on coming home, and as a Jamaican immigrant to America, I have, experienced de-coupled race related success. Like the people in Foner (1978); Lowenthal (1972); Waters (1999) and Vickerman (1999), previous to coming to America, I did not know what it truly meant to be black. In comparison to Britain and America, there are relatively no immediate observable social consequences to being a darker or lighter Jamaican. Waters (1999) cites Patterson who explains that in Jamaica, the belief in white superiority is minor and does not determine the way the people define themselves. Other researchers argue that skin color matters in Jamaica (Robotham 1998), but the ability to navigate the lines of demarcation are more fluid than in the USA and British societies where racism is structurally more restrictive.

While living in Jamaica during the 60s, 70s, and 80s, I witnessed the migration stream to foreign lands, but more often than not to America. The grapevine had it that migration to England was less desirable as many Jamaicans who migrated to England in the 1950s were mad, so poor they could not take a trip home, and the British Government was offering cash incentives to make West Indians leave. Such reports were never verified by return migrants but the physical appearance of return migrants from the US provided clues about their superior wealth, for they swanked, and careened around Jamaica in expensive rental cars which the populace could not afford. This view of return migrants from the US reinforced the research literature of that period, that Jamaicans were ethnic heroes doing extremely well in business (e.g., Glazer and Moynihan 1965).

What drew me to this study was my own experience with racism and reading Waters (1999) *Black Identities: West Indian dreams and American Realities*, and Vickerman (1999) *Crosscurrents*. Through their work I became aware of the structural obstacles which black migrants faced and how our Jamaican upbringing contributes to naiveté. As an extension of their work I am exploring how Jamaican cultural realties continue to shape migration and return migration.

Analyzing the Data

The life of an individual and the role played over an extended period in a community is best understood through life stories (Atkinson 1998). This information helps researchers to become more aware of how culture shapes one's life, the roles individuals play within communities and how roles change over time.

For the most part, I present each life story as a personal stand-alone document (Atkinson 1998). But, some life stories are edited into extracts so as to illustrate the effects of identity and mobility shifts on return migration. Spradley (1979) used such an approach, such that only 60% of the descriptions were actually the interviewee's own words and language.

In making sense of the scripts I asked myself, "now that I have these life stories how do I read and understand them?" In providing answers to this question I focused on finding the relevant information as it applied to migrants' shifts in socio-economic mobility and identity, and returnees and Jamaican countrymen perceptions of each other. This was a difficult task for the identity and socio-economic shifts occurred unconsciously—while migrants were doing things to accrue vital capital. However, as I listened to the returnees a common theme emerged in the data about race-based experience abroad and difficulties on returning to Jamaica. More importantly, I realized that interviewees were clear about their social differences previous to migrating and on returning home.

To sort through the information, I first looked for broad patterns across the data as it provided information about migration and return migration experiences and as it related to gaining entry into Britain and the U.S. and re-entry into Jamaican societies. I broke down the data into discrete parts showing the years spent abroad various reasons returnees had for migrating and returning to Jamaica; the economic achievements of returnees; the effects of returnees' bifocal transnational identity, and countrymen's and returnees' perceptions of each other. Ultimately I accounted for all of the material so that information about outlier cases was included.

I organized the data into returnees home and host country experiences, and the sex of interviewees. The reason for doing this was that migrants recognized that they came from different backgrounds, had different experiences that related to their Jamaican backgrounds and women's account of migration, and return migration were consistently different from men's. At first I was surprised by women's candid remarks, but found that this difference was supported by the literature.

Second, I looked at age of returnees because those who returned at a younger age saw themselves as being better adjusted than migrants who returned in later years.

Third, I looked at hierarchy, how group members showed allegiance to membership in their associations and to the president of associations; the interviews would not have been possible without the president's approval. Hierarchy was also established within the group of British return migrants by their house size. Noticing this I enquired about one returnee who lived in a ranch style house, and why his house was so small, I found out that he returned from America.

Fourth, I looked at Jamaican countrymen's perceptions of returnees' identity and mobility, and at the perceptions returnees held about their return and about countrymen. What I found was both had achieved economic success but in two different countries at the expense of their ethnicity, and familial bonds.

Fifth, I looked at what returnees did procedurally over the course of their lives to regain entry into Jamaican life, and the various institutions that were involved in their return process.

Characteristics of Interviewees

Most were born in rural parishes. The majority of voluntary migrants to the U.S. had at least a high school education at the time of migration, but those who went to England tended to have less than a high school education at the time of migration. It was relatively easy to trace the career paths of return migrants from the US, but it was difficult to place male migrants who went to England in any one job, as they moved frequently from job to job to avoid racism, and to achieve anticipated pensions. In contrast, women tended to be nurses. This movement did not affect their retirement as pensions came from the British government and in some cases from private investments. However, their occupations include: painter, carpenter, nurses, mechanic, welder, and postman.

At the time of conducting my first interview, all voluntary return migrants from England were receiving retirement pensions from the British government and on average returned to Jamaica within the last twenty years. Returnees from the U.S. had an average age of 40 to 50 years, but those from England were between 65 and 75 years of age.

Memory is vital to the process of collecting data through life stories. This issue was of concern to me as most of my subjects were elderly and some suffered from diabetes which might have impaired their memory. One way that ethnographers address the fallibility of human memory is to live among their subjects. But, this was not available to me as on each trip I had just three weeks to visit Jamaica.

To ensure some reliability, I asked the same question in different ways. For example, "what is your age" was asked in the second formatting, "in what year were you born again?" A second way that I ensured reliability was to ask in-depth questions on successive interviews that were held each December from 2004 to 2006. Each time I received the same story plot, but with more details. A good example was Olivive whose initial sessions yielded cursory information about her life in Jamaica, but in subsequent sessions spoke freely about her early sexual experiences.

I also held conversations with voluntary returnees across the island who belonged to different Associations of Returned Residents. Though I collected data from different settings the information is valid as each case contributed to my understanding of return migration (Becker 1998). I also spoke with return residents who were not members of any association so as to ensure that association members had not created a single script that was simply being repeated. I also consulted countrymen who served return residents. An example was a Mayor who spoke at a Returned Residents Association Christmas gathering in 2004. He was intimately involved with the activities of the town and was quite aware of the importance of returnee remittances, and their contribution to civil society in Jamaica. My prime confidants were friends in Jamaica and the acclaimed founder of the Returned Residents Association. Not knowing the ties which existed between returned migrants from Britain I assumed falsely that he was unaware of my planned interviewees with return migrants who were Association members. I have since identified him as the gate keeper to one faction of return migrants. It was through him that I gained access to interviewees in Clarendon.

List of Voluntary Return Migrants

Paul: I met Paul after I wrote to one chapter of the returned residents association seeking permission to conduct interviews with returnees. He was born in the parish of St. Thomas in Jamaica on August 7, 1941, and has been involved in several political and social organizations and activities aimed at creating a better life for those in need of representation.

In the mid 1950s he migrated to Birmingham in the United Kingdom where he pursued his vocational education and career in the field of Mechanical Engineering. He also created private businesses abroad and on returning to Jamaica.

Reg and June: I met Reg in the 1970s when he first returned from England, and enrolled his children in the primary school where my mother taught. Reg was married to June and came from the parish of Clarendon. They returned to England in search of greater income and a more equitable society. While in England he worked in the construction industry. In his final years, before returning to Jamaica, he managed to get building contracts for himself. But, in the midst of the projects his health failed due to an irregular heartbeat. On the advice of his doctor the projects were aborted. Unfortunately, he lost the money which was already invested in the buildings because the owners refused to reimburse his costs for partially completed buildings. This experience provided encouragement for him to returning to Jamaica in 1998.

Harold migrated to England in the 1950s, and returned to Jamaica in 1998. In England he held several labor jobs and could not believe that at long last he had retired and had more money than expected. He said, "I counted every day from the time I decided to retire, an' on the day after mi last day, mi wife had to call me back, I get ready for work and was waiting for the bus. They treated me nice on the job, the men got together and told me they would buy me anything that I wanted." Despite his wealth, he was bereft of intimate friendships.

Herby and Angella were married and migrated to England in the 1950s where Herby worked as a laborer and Angela as a nurse. They saved over the years and returned to Jamaica in 2003. They tried to help their own children in England by permitting them to "rent to own" their home but the children did not honor the agreement which affected their ability to complete their home in Jamaica. Both suffered with medical conditions, and so felt that Jamaica could be sweet if one returned with their health. This was a major issue because medicine consumed a major part of their retirement.

Merissa and Chad were married. Chad worked the land behind my mother's house in Jamaica and that is how I met the couple. He migrated to England in the 1950s and in 1961 she joined him—and they both returned in 1988 after Chad was diagnosed with lung cancer. Merissa was born in 1938, in Christiana—a town in the center of the island. There she went to All-Age School until age 15. In her words:

> I became pregnant with my first daughter because, parents during this time only beat children, and did not explain about the birds and the bees. I went to England because that's where the men that I met were going. Also, I went as a means of getting away from my parents—especially my father who called me terrible names because of my out-of-wedlock daughter.

John worked as a postal clerk and benefited from the agency's policy to offer early retirement packages to long standing employees who had health benefits and employ contract workers who would not be provided with these costly health benefits.

Winnie went to the U.S. with his father in the 1950s and returned to Jamaica in 1998 to fulfill his religious calling. But he did not feel that Jamaica was his final stop as Jamaicans were too difficult to get along with.

Cleveland migrated to England in 1950s and retuned in 1966. He was born in Kingston, Jamaica, and went to Mico Practicing Primary School at age 6, where his uncle was the headmaster. At age 11 he went to Excelsior High School, graduated at 17 and took his first job as a store clerk. He felt that he did not need to migrate to achieve a better life. He is my wife's godfather.

Victor knew my wife's grandparents and is the relative of a family friend. He was born on August 1, 1928 in an impoverished district named Sandy-Gutt (near Harewood), St. Catherine. His life story illustrates how improvements in the colonial capital element of education can shorten mid-colonial capital migrants' stay abroad, and help such migrants to have experiences that are almost like those who had high-colonial capital at the time of migration.

Franco: I lived in Franco's rental house for one year from 1988 to 1989. Franco first went to America as contracted farm labor to cut sugar cane. Eventually the company which contracted laborers liked his administrative skills and hired him permanently. He returned from America at age sixty-five to Jamaica in 1987. He owns a small farm and a rental home.

Dot: I went to the University of the West Indies with Dot and have maintained contact. She is a 47 year old teacher who migrated to America in 1986 to work and pursue a Masters degree. She returned from America in 2003 because she stated, "I was in Jamaica so often that it made sense to stay. When I did my final exam I came to Jamaica and completed it in a hotel." She lives in a rented house, owns minibuses and runs computer training centers. Since returning she worked as a Minister of Religion and as a high school teacher.

Goodwin: I went to high school with Goodwin and before migrating to the U.S. he taught at the primary school where my mother was principal. He said, "I had out grown America and was only accruing bills." Goodwin was a slightly built 43 years old male who lived in a rural district before migrating to Boston, Massachusetts in 1983 where he worked as a public school teacher, while being involved in secondary employment activities. For him there were only two kinds of Jamaicans in America, those who could return, and those who wanted to return—but could not for various reasons. He returned to his home town in 2003, to slowly construct his dream house over the course of 5 years. Whatever was his source of wealth, it permitted him to not seek for employment in Jamaica.

Hugh owned a gas station and said, "I went to America to earn money so as to make improvements to my business. To earn money abroad I worked in a water delivery business which grew under my supervision. I earned the respect and business of customers by making prompt deliveries" He was also Chairman of the local primary school board where he initiated computer skills training geared towards improving the skills of workers in the community.

Janice was a nurse who worked periodically in America, as she felt necessary to accomplish financial stability in Jamaica. Her longest stay in America was for six months.

List of Interviewed Deportees

Mark lives in the neighborhood where my mother bought her retirement home. He was an emblematic case of how the shifts in parental relationships portended deportation among children. He was born in the parish of Manchester (a rural area of Jamaica), but migrated to rejoin his parents in New York. He was one of 8 children who his mother filed for in 1986.

James: I met James through my contacts with the local police. His experiences illustrates that irreversible psychotic effects from drug use do accompany downward economic mobility and the harsh realities 1.5 generation adolescents faced. He was born in a district called "Picky Picky" in Manchester Jamaica, and migrated at the age of 14 to join his parents in New York City. Although he had 2 brothers and 2 sisters, he was the oldest and only child from the union of his mother and father.

Neville made an interesting comparison case as he migrated to the U.S. during his late twenties, after holding a permanent job in Jamaica. He worked for 20 years in the U.S. before being deported. He attributed deportation to activities which started in Jamaica.

Jay: I met Jay through a life long friend who has remained in Jamaica. Jay went to England on the invitation of his sister who intended to introduce him to the hardships of living abroad, but her intentions were not for him to stay. However, Jay saw this as his chance to earn some money. After all he had gone to England and so could not return without the trappings of wealth to satiate the expectations his local community had of return migrants. To circumvent the visitor visa laws Jay enrolled in a community college program, but was deported after attempting to find work.

Bobby: I met Bobby through Jay—both live in the same district. He migrated to England as a visitor, but started his own business after 4 weeks and was married within 3 months. For Bobby during these years it was possible for visitors to remain without much legal requirements as illegal immigration was not of paramount importance to English police. It was not until the arrival of "Yardy" gangs from Kingston that Jamaicans gained high negative social profiles in English society. Bobby would not admit to being deported but the community had other evidence.

Cecile: I met her through my contacts at a local poor relief shelter. She was a mentally impaired female who was deported after spending 20 years abroad. She went to the U.S. at age 16 after graduating from high school in Jamaica in 1981 to join my mother in New York with the hope of achieving foreign wealth. Instead, she achieved poverty and bad family experiences.

Chris is my relative. He spent twenty years in the U.S. before being deported. To his relatives he had not made use of his time but wasted his time and resources on a following of "big bottom American girls," who wanted nothing more than his money. To his relatives it was not of importance that Chris sold drugs, but that he did not have the transnational sense to save some of the lucre in a Jamaican bank. From Chris's standpoint, his drug sales in the U.S. were not substantial enough to open a bank account in Jamaica while selling drug in New York.

Rudolph migrated to the U.S. and returned to his parents' home but his cousin called the police after Rudolph tried to cut down a banana tree. Consequently he moved to the city of Montego Bay where life on the streets was particularly miserable as he had to sleep in homeless shelters.

Joseph was an outlier to the patterns found among deportees, as he owned his home but ate lunch at the parish food pantry. Joseph met his American wife in Jamaica, married her and moved to America. Eventually their marijuana use led to cocaine addiction, and his deportation.

Olivive: I met her through my contact at one of the local poor relief centers. She was another outlier case among deportees because she had one year of college, knew how to use the computer and the welfare program in Montego Bay has bought one for her to do some administrative tasks at the homeless shelter. During the days rather than loaf, she sold mirrors.

Samuel was born in my hometown in Jamaica where my mother taught him in primary school. Abroad he experienced a sharp decline in mobility after he started selling marijuana. His willingness to do anything for money was symbolized in a motto, "If the information applies, hitch on, but if it does not apply, then let it fly." After migrating he quickly opened up new marijuana supply corridors to Haitians and Puerto Ricans from Florida, Texas and New York, but was deported because of kidnapping charges.

Summarization of Chapters

Chapter One: "Introduction," works through the rationale for doing the research, developments in return migration theory and data collection. The book is concerned with exploring the life stories of return migrants and how their colonial capital at the time of migration differentiates them, and affects their migration experiences and re-entry into home societies where they are indistinguishable by race from the general population. The sociological and theoretical implications of colonial capital are wide ranging; it provides a firm basis for constructing a theory which explains deportees, and enables researchers to make precise predictions about migrants who share a common ethnicity.

Chapter Two: "Silly Me for Thinking Migration Would Overcome Colonial Prejudices," exposes the lives of two categories of voluntary return migrants— namely those with mid- and high-colonial capital. These life stories provide the reader with data for evaluating one core point in my research, that there are different categories of migrants and Transnational Theory only applies to those who left Jamaica with mid-colonial capital. Although all share a common ethnicity, yet they have different outcomes based on their colonial capital at the time of migration. The life story of Reg is used to illustrate patterns found among mid-colonial returnees and how efforts to achieve higher socio-economic status through migration can fall apart. They remained abroad 30 to 40 years to earn fuller pensions, but on returning home were subjected to poor reception, preyed upon by criminals who were sometimes their own relatives, and out rightly rejected by countrymen. To comfort their plight, these mid-colonial migrants engaged in transnational activities by forming similar association to the ones they use to resist English racism. This approach appropriately closed boundaries to outsiders, while forging protective ethnic housing, and church communities which ultimately strengthened personal wealth, and galvanized their self-identity. Although returnees felt comforted by each other, yet the thought of being rejected by countrymen was painful—like being among the English in the 1950s.

The life story of Cleveland illustrates the almost bland experiences of voluntary return migrants who had high-colonial capital at the time of migration. Such migrants did not have to leave Jamaica to achieve a better life, but went abroad to broaden world views, pursue opportunities not available in Jamaica, and then returned after 7 years. They had little or no need to negotiate obstacles by closing their ethnic boundaries to outsiders through imported systems, because they left Jamaica with the needed colonial capital to accomplish set goals over a short period of time, and their attitudes earned them respect even when faced with racism. Use of appropriate social graces was a significant element which distinguished migrants with high-colonial capital from those with mid-colonial capital. This will be explored more in depth in Chapter Four where migrants' paths are compared.

At the end of the chapter, excerpts illustrate returnees and countrymen's perceptions of each other. Together these perspectives help to identify: a) the unexpected dissonance between mid-colonial capital returnees' sense of their own identities as true Jamaicans and how they were identified by other Jamaicans; and, b) the complex ways in which return migrants' experiences and perception of their colonial capital were linked to changes in Jamaican society and shifts in the identity and mobility of countrymen.

Chapter Three: "You look Like A Fool Coming Home with Nothing: Involuntary Return Migrants" examines the life stories of involuntary return migrants (deportees). Analysis of their life stories further substantiates the need for a new migration theory, and the significance of colonial capital as a predictor variable of migrants' experiences. From a theoretical stand point it can be argued that deportees' return migration experiences were directly affected by their extremely low initial colonial capital. Other associated factors helped to bring about their decline such as poor parental supervision, their mental incapacity, involvement in drug peddling activities which deterred their mobility, and some were too young to construct their own success abroad.

The life stories of Mark, James, Neville, Samuel and Olivive, in particular, illustrate deportees' complex experiences. Upon returning to Jamaica they lacked wealth, and were excluded from community life, access to jobs, and the rungs of middle class Jamaican society; because of their stigmatized identities and lack of economic mobility. Part of the Jamaican norm is the expectation that return migrants should bring home enough wealth to be independent of public sector employment, create business and most of all provide demonstrable evidence by building large multi-storied houses. Meeting these expectations did not confer any permanent status, as return migrants had to be always ready to meet the demands of other Jamaicans who needed money on the spur of the moment.

As a consequence of these rites of passage in which deportees could not participate, they were denied the opportunity to negotiate re-entry into Jamaican society. Instead deportees lived on the edge of social activities and relationships. The boundaries of deportee activities were maintained through high levels of scrutiny which local communities applied. This close scrutiny robbed deportees of the freedom to implement transnational ideas, or invent stories which heightened their social esteem among peers.

Chapter Four: "Colonial Capital Matters: A Comparison of Voluntary and Involuntary Return Migrants" revisits the life stories from previous chapters, and focuses on the pattern of activities migrants performed. I first look at voluntary return migrants with mid- and high-colonial capital, and compare their activities with deportees. The patterns are then be used to improve the theoretical understandings about return migrants and especially deportees; a group slighted in return migration literature.

Excerpts of life stories show that although racism was a formidable structure, migrants with high-colonial capital used their education, family support, and especially their social graces to cut successful paths. A striking example of the importance of social graces is seen in the life stories of a returnee with mid-colonial capital cutting off the necktie of a bartender who refused to serve him. But, migrants with high-colonial capital when confronted with racism did not use physical force and were more tactful.

When the paths of mid-colonial capital migrants and those with the lowest colonial capital are compared, a revision of social psychology from Adler (1985:84) sums up of their different paths:

> When the lofty Jamaican dreams of [deportees] encountered the stark reality of economic decline in inner cities, [they had little colonial capital to draw upon] and took to drug wheeling and dealing which provided an opportunity to live for the present with the maximum pleasures they could grab. They temporarily achieved entrenched Jamaican childhood dreams by escaping the unpleasant responsibilities of life abroad, and seizing the opportunity to surround themselves with anything money could buy.

In contrast, mid-colonial capital migrants transferred helpful cooperative strategies from Jamaica such as Pardner, formed ethnic associations, and earned pensions over 30 to 40 years while saving miniscule sums of money.

Chapter Five: "Conclusion" provides provocative conclusive statements, and looks at an important weakness which should guide future research. The chief weakness has to do with the fact that the sample does not contain cases of financially successful deportees. Some such persons do exist, but they may have gained upward mobility through illegal activities and this makes them unlikely candidates for life story interviews. Second, colonial capital is confounded with age at the time of returning to Jamaica and with the length of time migrants spent overseas. Future studies need to have a sample with more variation in years spent away and in age at the time of return for people who hold various levels of colonial capital.

Although the modest sample size does not permit generalization, the results generated in Chapter Two strongly suggests that there are at least two categories of voluntary return migrants—one with high-colonial capital and the other with mid-colonial capital. Deportees who had the least colonial capital were homeless, suffered most from alienation, and denial of re-entry into Jamaican communities, as the building of luxury houses was an integral rite of passage. Those deportees who returned to live in family homes, and had skills, still suffered rejection from the community because they had not built their own homes to meet social expectations associated with migration.

This research helps to clarify West Indian return migration literature which suggests that engagement in transnationalism is a given for all West Indian returnees. Based on this research, I argue that Transnational Theory best applies to migrants with mid-colonial capital who remained abroad for 30 to 40 years.

Currently, return migration theories (e.g., NCE, NELM, Structuralism and Transnational Theory) apply only to voluntary return migrants. Hence, there is demand for new theories to apply when immigrants are deported and prohibited by force of law from carrying out the presumed cycle of arrival and departure in similar fashion to voluntary return migrants. To contribute to the development of a more comprehensive theoretical explanation of return migration experiences, I argue that: return migration and transnational experiences are based on the migrants' Jamaican colonial capital at the time of migrating, and time away from home.

In my research, the effects of colonial capital were robust, as in each society to which migrants moved, they faced prejudices about their colonial capital, and so discovered unwanted continuities or inferior roles that they thought had been left abroad. In the case of voluntary returning migrants who remained abroad to earn full pensions, their colonial capital shared a positive relationship with declining effect on their migration and return migration experiences. That is, their bi-focal identity and the transfer of financial capital helped them at first to gain limited entry into foreign societies and Jamaican society. But they were denied full acceptance because of the prejudices countrymen held about other important elements of colonial capital such as lighter skin, formal education, and social graces. In essence their money did not buy everything.

One element that returnees' wealth did not change was their skin color. This sociological reality, lead some male return migrants to take the next best action, and marry lighter skinned women. Clearly such action could not improve the personal colonial capital of the migrants, but showed, at least, that they made some attempt. The colonial capital of migrants with the highest colonial capital who returned after remaining between 7 to 15 years abroad (education, family support and acquisition of social graces) shared a positive relationship with migration and return migration experiences. Abroad they suffered little shift in their identity, but achieved educational and financial mobility. On returning to Jamaica they quickly resettled without being involved in transnationalism. This research points to the need for researchers to be sensitive to the significance of colonial capital in explaining the outcomes of migrants of African ancestry; all of their experiences do not have to do with race alone.

CHAPTER TWO
Silly Me for Thinking Migration Would Overcome Colonial Prejudices

Sweet Jamaica
Land that we love
How I long for her shores.

The above excerpt came from a poem titled "Sweet Jamaica" and was written and read by a member of the Returned Residents Association in Mandeville, Jamaica. Each December the members organize a formal dinner function to celebrate returning, and accrue money which is donated to worthy causes. While "Sweet Jamaica" summed up the joy of returning, especially after working in menial jobs, and enduring cold weather abroad, it carefully avoided any mention of the prejudices some returnees faced among countrymen who told them "nobody can come change Jamaica, go back where you came from" and that these unexpected challenges made returnees question the sweetness of Jamaica.

During the 1950s mid-colonial capital returnees migrated to England so as to emerge from poverty and achieve white colonial standards of living within 5 years (Olwig 1988). But, they had to remain longer because their colonial capital at the time of migration placed them at the bottom of the British socio-economic hierarchy and this predicament was exacerbated by institutionalized racism.

To resist racism, migrants forged appropriate relationships by being cordial to all despite race, while importing helpful cooperative systems from Jamaica, which involved only Jamaicans. This approach appropriately closed their ethnic boundaries to outsiders, forged protective ethnic housing, and church communities which ultimately strengthened their personal wealth, and galvanized their self-identity. The efforts of migrants to find rooms to rent were assisted by savvy English property owners, who saw that there was money to be made from renting blacks rooms in buildings selected to be torn down. Yet, some were given government owned "council flats" which they used to gain economic mobility by further subletting rooms to other West Indians migrants. The accrued capital was combined with payoffs from their informal banking system called "Pardner" to purchase homes in which they continued the practice of living in a small section and renting out the rest of rooms. In Pardner, small groups of Jamaicans gave pre-determined sums to one person—called a banker. At pre-determined intervals each person in the group would take turns receiving the total pool of money—called a hand. British Banks did not understand this system for banks paid interest on savings but Pardners did not. However, the advantage was that when the hand was drawn there was no need for a loan from British financial institutions, which did not support Jamaican migrants anyway (Phillips and Phillips 1998).

Living together provided the freedom to maintain ethnic habits which were reminiscent of home, such as keeping house parties and church services with loud laughter and lively music. But, their English neighbors and landlords routinely called the police to impose noise ordinances. Although migrants still thought of themselves ethnically as true Jamaicans, it was in their best interest to replace or tone down ethnic habits which reinforced their racial inferiority, and threatened their new found source of wealth in housing. This was one way in which migrants adjusted themselves to be like native born persons (Waldinger 2006), for they realized that, home ownership was seminal to their mobility abroad, and in Jamaica. On leaving England some migrants sold homes that were bought in the 1950s for £5,000 for up to £80,000 in the 1990s. The accrued sales profit was used as capital for completing luxury homes in Jamaica.

Not withstanding the harsh realities of being denied access to housing, jobs and social activities, migration to England was a step towards economic mobility and away from the lack of opportunities in Jamaica (Bennett 2002). But as migrants gained mobility through home ownership in different cities, inadvertently friendships weakened because home owners rarely saw those who remained in government flats and rented rooms.

This shift set the tone of Jamaican migrants' lives in that they achieved the migrants' dream of financial mobility, but they substituted their ethnic habits with quasi-English ways in order to fit into English communities. Although mid-colonial migrants had made these strides, they did not mix well with the English, as improvement in their social graces colonial capital element was necessary.

On returning to Jamaica, life was sweet as mid-colonial capital returnees built dream homes to establish that they had overcome lower class boundaries. But by and large they were still dark skinned persons who lacked college degrees and lost the necessary social graces to mix well with countrymen.

In reaction to the rejection of countrymen, returnees retreated by living in housing enclaves that were located far away from their communities of origin. Belonging to and returned residents associations also helped to soothe their anger and frustration about returning home. Below is an illustrative life story from Reg—periodically he came to see my mother who taught his children after he took them back to Jamaica.

Reg's Story

In 1932 I was born in a little district called Lodgie Green. My mother was a housewife, and my father was a farmer of yams, banana, sugar cane, and he also reared cattle. My mother had 3 children before marrying, and their union produced 5 children: 3 girls; and two boys. After marrying she took me to live with her new husband, since I was the last of the first three children; the two older siblings remained with their father who was a good man.

At the time land was rented from two "big backras" who were the white property owners, and then the government of Jamaica bought the lands and turned them into settlements. The government did this because renting land from backras did not provide security for the settlers to plant long term crops like coconuts, or build permanent concrete homes.

Before going to England in 1958, life was very tough economically in Jamaica. At the time there was a market for all farm produce. Milk was sold to a condensery, and ground food was sold to entrepreneurs, who after buying the produce from us, transported it to Kingston from the nearby train station in Frankfield. Banana was shipped, and the sugar cane was sold to a local factory. The income was regular as the condensery paid us for the milk every fortnight. But it was not enough to acquire the life I have now. As poor people, we were happy with our provision of daily food from the farm. Our main concern was to have money to pay doctor's bill, and the necessary clothes in preparation for an accident. If there were an accident, necessitating medical care, neighbors would take it as their responsibility to ask for the doctor's money, and the hospital clothes. If the money was loaned out, the borrower would repay it quickly.

I went to Grantham Kilsyth Elementary School at 7 years old. Before going to school I did not think about differences among people, but on going to school I observed immediately that light skinned children were treated better than dark skinned children. I later saw this in my town where children who looked Chinese, white, and brown were treated differently from black children. My mother's relatives were light skinned, although she was a dark skinned Maroon. As a result of my relatives' skin color and status, although I was a dark skinned person, I did not suffer as much ill treatment as other dark skinned children who had no fair skinned relatives. This sense of protection gave me an incentive to cling to light skinned and white people. I made up my mind from age 7 to improve the life of my children by marrying a fair skinned woman, and did so at age 26.

My elementary school had different grades starting with A, then B, junior class and then 1st class upward to 6th standard. At the end of elementary school one could do an additional 2 years to prepare for taking 1st, 2nd and 3rd year Jamaica Local Exams. Sixth standard prepared students for farming, manual labor jobs, and being a police officer, or a pupil teacher. First and Second Year Local Exams prepared students for entry level careers, like being an assistant postal clerk. Third Year Local Exams prepared students for fully fledged upper level positions in careers such being a post mistress. I stopped going to school at 6th standard because I could not afford the cost of books and education.

The year 1951 was a turning point in my life as I left school and went into farming hoping this would be my final profession. I combined my 6th standard qualification, which was a fairly good education, along with the practical experience gained from seeing my father tending to the cattle, and entered farm-ing. But, I noticed that one could not make enough money from farming. This was most evident after the 1951 hurricane which flattened every crop, and drowned animals. As a farmer I was left standing just like Alice in Wonderland—with nothing. The hurricane was the first devastating blow to me as a young farmer, that's when I noticed that the only people making money were those with a trade.

At age 19 I decided to pick up cabinet making at my cousin's shop in Grantham. My cousin's furniture manufacturing shop occupied one room on the lower floor of a two story board building. He was the main furniture maker in town who brought a wealth of knowledge about making furniture from having worked in Kingston (the capital city of Jamaica) to rural Grantham.

I can remember the transition from being a farmer to a worker dressed up in khaki uniform with shined boots. There was another boy who worked for my cousin, but I had preference, because I was the owner's cousin and a member of an extended family that had high color and status. My job duties were to first sweep out the store, and then learn woodwork by pushing a wood plane and using the manual saw to cut wood accurately. Developing the art of sawing was a slow process which helped furniture makers to avoid becoming tired. Although it makes sense now, back then I felt that my cousin did not push me ahead and that he did not want me to make furniture too quickly.

This apprenticeship to my cousin lasted for about one year. The shop was too much of a confinement after having grown up on a farm. Also while learning woodwork I was paying workers to do work on my farm and I was supporting myself from the farm proceeds (my cousin did not pay me much; if anything at all).

It was about 1956 when I left and went into building construction with a contractor who was known to train many boys. The system in Jamaica was an English styled apprenticeship where students worked with a local authority or a skilled professional for a time and then moved on to create their own business. I brought my accuracy in using a saw, plane and chisel from making furniture to constructing buildings. The first day of work I was paid as the contractor saw that I could do his work very well. One memorable house is still standing today that I helped to construct.

Each week I received 2 shillings and 6 pence. This income along with income from my farm meant that I was like a big shot with plenty of money, and I was partially an employer; which was one of my ambitions. Life was good, as when the construction trade was slow I sold oranges, sugar cane, cows, and pigs. I was among the elite as I bought my first bicycle and built a 2 room concrete house on the 1 acre of settlement land I bought from the government through my father. I also built my own furniture for my home.

I fulfilled my childhood prediction and got married at age 26 to my wife who came from Mandeville but grew up in my district with her aunt. I planned my family, how many children, and how far away from home I should take jobs. I was now the local builder.

My first child was born in 1959. I had a second child as this was part of our plan. I did not want to leave Jamaica, but all of my elementary school books, called *Caribbean Readers* were about England. Further my cousin who had migrated encouraged me, and this was where others were going to seek for fortune and fame; but I always said no. Even my cousin with whom I learned furniture building was already in England.

One day after coming home from the field in the rain I just decided to go. I came home, told my wife about my decision and later that year left for London.

My first job as a carpenter joiner with the Council ended after 2 years because the Council building project finished, and the Council jobs were now being outsourced to private contractors.

My second job as a structural carpenter was with Wimpy, one of the biggest construction companies in England. This was welcomed growth as my pay increased to between £18 and £25 per week, and each task was priced. On my second job, at Wimpy, working conditions improved as I was now assimilated into English culture and understood slang words. I was also going to Willesden Technical College where I learned to sketch frames, and then build them. I spent 2 years there. Two major constructions I was a part of, were the Center Point building in London, and the London Bridge Project.

I was also comfortable in my church and went to Bible College. My knowledge of church was so much that I could help others to interpret the Bible, and it helped me to learn how to interact with others who suffered problems at work and at home. I was always like a counselor.

In February of 1962 when my wife joined me in England, she worked fulltime in a factory making lamps and for a short period as 3rd shift nursing assistant—she left this because the night shift was too taxing. We did not have any outright personal racist experiences in England, but were denied work and housing. I remember having to live in one bedroom apartments. Blacks could not find enough rooms to rent because most English people would not permit blacks to live in their houses. Sometimes rooms were advertised but when we showed up the owners said they were already rented. But, when whites went they were able to rent these same rooms. To get rooms, Jamaicans asked whites friends to sublet rooms and then blacks sneaked in at night. Those Jamaicans who went up in the early 1950s were lucky enough to rent rooms in dilapidated buildings that were slated to be torn down. These lucky Jamaicans then rented to others who came later. Sometimes there were six people in one room taking turns to sleep. Some slept in the day and went to work at night and those who worked at night slept in the day.

Since blacks were excluded from social activities, these rooms served for our private social activities, dining room, living room and bedroom. After work we bought liquor and food, and visited each other's room. As Jamaicans all over, we would sit and talk, play cards, and we loved loud music—but the landlord would call the police. This was one example of how living in England forced changes in Jamaican habits.

On Sundays these same rooms were used for church. If there were not enough chairs then each visitor brought their own chair. As the number of children grew, we moved from living in one rooms, to government council flats which provided 2 and 3 rooms, private bathrooms/kitchen, and then into detached houses. The detached houses back then could cost as little as £4,000. We helped each other to save the down payment on homes by throwing Pardner. My weekly wage was only £5, and out of this income I sent money to care for my children who were left with my parents in Jamaica, paid my living expenses in England, government National Insurance, and saved. Sometimes I wonder how we did so much with so little. When I think about all of the hardships, nobody in Jamaica should grudge us for what we have. I was a settled family man and started to think about owning my own apartment with my own key. I bought my first house on Yewfield Road in the same Willesden area of London from my savings. I lived in Willesden in 1965 from until 1972. It was a mixed neighborhood and we were the second black family to move there; not many came after. I did not have to do anything special to save money to purchase this house because from the day I left school I was industrious and refused to stay where I was financially. My first house was a terrace house with 2 stories, and 3 bedrooms. We were the only black family on the whole block. I bought my first car too, it was a Riley Woolsey. It was a joy to pick up my wife from work and drive to work. This was an improved living. When homes were bought, the friendships formed in one rooms broke because some bought homes outside of London and in different cities and in the country parts, and we felt more accepted by whites and other blacks. Now, the only time we saw old friends was when we visited each other on special occasions. But owning our homes provided more rooms for later Jamaican migrants, as we rented out rooms. Bathrooms and kitchens were shared.

At age 26, I planned on returning to Jamaica in 10 years with enough money to establish myself. But I was also worried over my children after going to their school and observing that black children could do as they wanted. I remember the day that I decided to come home. It was end of term open-day at my daughter's school. One teacher asked my wife, what is your child like at home? White people are like that, they are not real smart, but they play on what others say. My wife said that my daughter was head strong. The teacher then said, "Some days she does not want to do any work, then on another day she will do her work willingly. On those days that she doesn't want to work I let her do as she wants." I said to my wife we are going home. I put my house on the market, stored the furniture for a month and shipped to Jamaica.

Returning to Jamaica prematurely, solved the problem of good elementary education for children, but mid-colonial returnees faced questions about their mobility, as they did not bring sizeable fortunes. To insulate themselves against archaic expectations of grandeur, migrants returned abroad to earn full pensions and enough resources to resettle outside of their Jamaican communities of origin. Despite their best efforts, when mid-colonial capital returnees later came home permanently, they still faced the absolute envy of countrymen, and the annoying reports that not even one's relatives were to be trusted, as they were, on occasion, the perpetrators of crimes against returnees.

In reaction to these pervasive fears mid-colonial capital returnees tried to build good relationships by buying groceries for the needy, giving away more money than countrymen solicited, and by joking with countrymen. Returnees also simultaneously closed rank against countrymen by belonging to return residents associations, churches, and home owners associations. This forged protective enclaves within which returnees galvanized their self-identity as the benchmark of discipline and success. Within these closed boundaries, mid-colonial capital return residents provided themselves with the social activities they had grown accustomed while living abroad. Periodically, fully pensioned mid-colonial capital return migrants visited England for medical care, to see friends and family, and to break the monotony of living among countrymen in rural Jamaica. But being friendly and belonging to private groups and transnational activities did not protect mid-colonial capital migrants from inner disappointments about their dark skin. With all of their years of work and wealth, some mid-colonial capital returnees felt that their dark skin was a social impediment and the reason that wealthy brown skinned business owners did not socialize with them beyond cordial business conversations.

Reg's Story in Jamaica

In Jamaica I moved in with my wife's parents who were happy to have us. On arriving in Jamaica in 1972, I settled my children in Kylsiths Primary School— this was back to my roots. I also lined out my house in Kylsiths but one afternoon just changed my mind. Then my brother came and told me that the local shop keeper had a lot of land for sale in Spaldings. I wrote a check immediately without seeing the lot. The owner was so happy that he thought my check was full payment for the lot, but I said no that it was just a deposit.

My wife asked me how I was going to manage in Jamaica without finding work—but if I could not find someone to take care of the children; I made up my mind to remain. After 13 months in Jamaica my children were fully settled in school and luckily I was able to board my children with relatives I realized that my passport was gold because my friends wished for the opportunities I had in England and here I was sitting on a passport. That wasn't right as I could use this passport to help my friends to survive. I went back to England and stayed with friend and then with my cousin.

I went back to my 3rd job in England as a subcontractor. This second tenure lasted for 2 years until I joined Bovis as a carpenter. I remained with Bovis until about 2 years before I returned to Jamaica. The recession came and Bovis lost work. After Bovis, I subcontracted on my own and formed my own refurbishing construction. Just as I was about to branch out in construction with my own contracts and running simultaneous crews, the last three jobs in England took me under. I was unable to deliver the houses because the doctor advised me to quit working or face the possibility of dying. I did not know that people could be so difficult. Although the houses were 80% complete the owners still would not accept them, or give me back the money that I had invested. I swore never to build another house again.

I came home for the second and final time in 1997, but my wife came in 1999 because she was still on the work force earning her pension. In the early years she worked full time and could afford to make the necessary NIS contributions to earn a full pension. But, when more children came along she could only work part time and this lowered her pension contributions. In the final 13 years she worked with the local government helping elderly people. This full time job provided the needed funds to make up for the previous short fall in NIS contributions and helped her to get a full government pension in 1999.

During my time with Bovis I sent money home and my house was already built from 1973 to provide boarding accommodations for the nearby high school and community college students.

Boarding is a lifelong dream come true from 12 years of planning. Boarding has created an immediate family as the children see me as Dad. This money I don't really need as I get my pension from England too. I have used my house as a refuge to the community and for students who cannot pay and many times I give free boarding to students who cannot afford it.

I also farm, to produce food instead of having to buy. Boarding and farming have made me an employer, which was another dream come true. People are not always grateful for the contributions I have made. Like you board students, and they don't pay and in farming people don't pay for the goods. Jamaicans are not trustworthy and like to spite returnees. For example, I went into farming but could not get any market for the goods; the people blocked me as a returnee. The people that I depended on did not help me. In one case I rented a piece of land and the owner also planted crops there too. He promised to get me an order, but twice he made excuses. Eventually, I went to his field at an odd time and found him digging yams for the promised buyer.

I abandoned that farm and went to Lodgie Green among my nephews and brothers. But it was just the same, they only helped when I spent money to plant. When they needed markets they got it, and sold their stuff when I was not around. Because I could not do the reaping, each time I walked away and all the money invested went down the drain. I get respect from people but no support at the point when I am looking for returns, it is as if they pull the carpet. I then went to farm in Ballieston, near to where I have formed a new Pentecostal church. Members now support my farming venture by preparing the land, planting the crops and finding the markets. I don't look at negatives I move on, and whatever I set out to do nothing stops me.

Farming is what I know, and that is the contribution I can make. This is not possible in carpentry. For example, I put in a letter to the principal to do free carpenter's labor. The letter was passed on, and I was supposed do 2 half day's as a contribution, but the head staff claimed I was coming to take away their jobs. But some contributions are possible in farming, when I give away food and people say thanks.

Crime, that is the biggest problem in Jamaica, and to tackle this obstacle, I don't let anyone past my front porch; that goes for relatives too. In many cases of crime against returned residents, it is their own relatives that set up other people to come and rob them. For example, in England I lived side by side with a returnee who returned to live among her brother and his son who cut her throat because they said she was too mean. Returnees have 3 M's to spell their name—they are mad, they are mean and they have money.

One has to be diplomatic as all Jamaicans want is money. No brother or sister; none come in this house to scrutinize it. I have one house cleaner and some parts of the house she does not go. If a relative comes to visit I take them to this porch.

I still try to get along with the community. I am of the opinion that it is not only Jamaicans who think that returned residents are strangers, but returned residents make themselves into strangers. I try to get along by living among the people. When I go in the market I run a little joke with the ladies. If somebody asks for money I give them and say, "here is some more give it to your friend too." If I am buying groceries I buy extra for somebody else in the community, give money and groceries to the needy. Jamaicans, I don't trust them and if I loan someone money I don't expect repayment.

I recognize that there are limits to my success. Although I received a British Empire medal in 1987 for contribution to the building industry, and Union of Construction Trade and Technicians, letters of contribution to St. Paul's Cathedral which permit baptisms and marriages at the Cathedral for 3 generations, if I were brown then my life would be better. When you look around you see evidence of this. My wife was told in England that she was different because she was a brown person and so was able to provide better care for her patients.

Here in Spaldings town, businesses have shut down yet the only store to survive is owned by a fair skinned Jamaican. If you go down to the two hardware stores in town, the one owned by the black person is a different store than the store owned by the mulatto. I realize that mulatto store owners have respect for my money, but they would not invite me home for dinner.

Life among Jamaicans can become monotonous and that is one purpose of belonging to a returned residents association where those who are kind of lost can meet those who know their experiences and can hold a conversation about other problems than money. I was introduced to the returning residents associations through my dorm house mother—she was the secretary. The president of the association was a teacher at her school. I joined in 1997. Membership cost JA$800. The association provides friendships with some migrants that I knew before leaving Jamaica and some friendships I have constructed. For example, I knew the current president of my returned resident's association before leaving Jamaica and she delivered my children in England. In returned residents associations there is a common understanding between us. After having been away from Jamaica for 40 years we have lost friendships. Since it takes a while to re-develop friendships, this association serves as a central meeting place.

The backlash effects from returnees' shifts in identity and mobility were very evident among migrants who belonged to returned residents associations but were still dissatisfied, and among pensioned migrants who felt they could not afford the cost of belonging to associations or transnational travel abroad. Harold exemplified the predicament of not gaining satisfaction from associating with return residents to play dominoes, eat prepared lunches, and take periodic trips across Jamaica and to other Caribbean islands. He reported below that he was disconnected from his real friends and community.

I spent 45 years in England and had 45 different jobs. Sometimes I wish if I could meet one of my old buddies from school days, someone I used to run with and that I really know. Although I come to the [returned resident's] association meetings there is no friendliness and intimacy. I really don't know anybody; everybody is new to me.

In England Harold held low paying laborer jobs which did not permit the luxury of frequent travel to Jamaica. After returning to Jamaica he realized that important ties with childhood friends were lost and for all of his financial gains abroad he was a lonely stranger among fellow pensioned returned migrants.

A second case known to this author was Adaco. He told his family, on one of the many occasions they asked for money, not to write or call him. After twenty years he returned home and went to look for his mother, but was told that she had died. He said, "I promptly asked why nobody told me?" Adaco reported, "my relatives said that they complied with my directive to not write or call." Adaco said he protested, "That's not what I meant." But, the damage was already done, he had learned to close his boundaries in England to achieve mobility but the extent of closure was at the expense of intimacy with his extended family and his mother who were in Jamaica.

Merrisa

The experiences of Merissa represent mid-colonial capital migrants who faced the rejection of countrymen, but felt that her pension was not large enough, to afford the succor of belonging to a returned residents association. Although Merissa lived in England for 27 years, and worked as an assistant nurse, both she and her husband, while he was alive, claimed to not have enough money. Merissa received JA$102,000 per month from National Insurance and widow's pension. In addition she received a full pension from her nursing career. Both Merissa and her husband received all health care in Jamaica and have not been back to England since returning home. Like three other women in the sample, Merissa preferred life abroad and had bitter complaints about the freedoms of her husband.

Merissa's Story

I went to England in 1961 and returned in 1988. I was born in 1938 in Christiana; a town in the center of the island where I went to All Age School until 15. I became pregnant with my first daughter because, parents during this time only beat children they did not explain why they were beating them and did not explain about the birds and the bees. I went to England because that's where the men that I met were going. Also, I went as a means of getting away from my parents and especially my father who called me terrible names because of the out of wedlock daughter.

There weren't many social activities except for community wide happenings on holidays like Johnkunoo on Christmas, yet children felt happy. Life was confined to staying at home and taking care of household chores. Although my father was a farmer, the tradition of the time forbade me from cultivating. My mother went to the market to sell the agricultural produce but girls were only allowed to do the shopping. It was on one of these shopping expeditions that I met boys and eventually my husband who was a farmer and painter. He left for England after making his love known to my parents. He went to live with his cousins rent free for the first 9 months. After that he gave them his money to save. It is some of this saving that he used to buy my ticket.

In 1961 I flew from Norman Manley Airport on British Airways. Daddy had a friend with a car, and that's how the family traveled to the airport. I arrived in London exhausted and remember the deep cold I felt and wanting to return to Jamaica. When you sweat it's like icicle on your skin. My husband came to meet me and had brought a winter coat. We went to Lloyd Street in Birmingham to live in one room, containing a paraffin heater, a bed, and 2 chairs—it was cold. The following month I went to the Exchange and signed on for work—it did not take long to get one. My first job was making Cadbury's chocolate. The workforce at the factory was mixed with English, Irish, Pakistani, Africans, and Jamaicans, and other West Indians. Working conditions involved being reprimanded for doing what others thought we should not have done. We were called Darkeys, Nigger and Monkey. I took a bus in the mornings to reach work by 8:00 a.m., and if I was late, money was deducted from my wages. When I came home to Jamaica it was surprising to see people not being punctual. I left work at 4:00 p.m. and took the bus home. Sometimes I walked home if I felt like it. My wages were £4 per week, until I reached age 21; then I was then paid £7 per week. It was the law in England that one could not get married in England under age 19 and that is why we came home to Jamaica to get married. After becoming pregnant I worked up to the 7th month of pregnancy. By law women did not return to work until after the baby was 4 months old. After giving birth, I did not return to that job but came to Jamaica in 1964 and got married.

After getting married we went to London because most of my husband's relatives lived there and everybody wanted him to come to London. The rooms were now bigger and we rented 2 bedrooms to accommodate the baby at 138 St James Road, West Croyden. I placed the baby in a nursery each morning and picked him up in the evenings. My husband worked then at a laundry. Money was not enough but the little we had was saved in the Jamaica Mutual Building Society in Jamaica. I bought the grocery and he paid the rent; in everything we went 50/50.

We did not join any Pardner to save money. Our first home was a council house which was given to us because we were not living in suitable conditions. After 5 years we had the option to purchase this and did so in the 1970s. Under Margaret Thatcher she afforded us limitless opportunities—the former prime minister did not permit this. To buy the council house, we paid down about £50,000 and then our rent was the mortgage; rent was about £500 per month. We sold the Council house after 5 years and bought 109 Pemdevom Road. This house had 3 bedrooms, internal plumbing, zero line lot line and was semi-detached. The passage between homes allowed the garbage to be removed from the back of homes.

Nursing was my second job and this started in 1971. This is what I wanted to do. I applied to the nursing council in Croyden, and started my training in this same year. Classes were held at the Mayday Hospital 5 days per week. As a pupil nurse I went to classes for 4 full months without working on the hospital ward. I then did 2 months on the ward, then went back to classes for one full month, and then back to the ward. After a final month of studying, I sat a conclusive test to gain certification as a State Registered Nurse. Exam results took a month to be published, but I still worked on the wards. Only one of my students failed.

My first full fledged nursing position was as a state registered nurse. I then did my midwifery training for 1 month. I wanted to do my psychiatric nursing and did it for 2 week but failed the exam, and did not try again. I stayed at Mayday Hospital until I came home to Jamaica, but I was still sent out to other hospitals when these hospitals were short of staff.

During the first 18 years in England my now husband worked as a painter taking home £200 to £300 per week. Work was good and steady, but difficult. Eventually he took an easier job as a hospital porter and retired from this position after 10 years due to illness. He liked being a porter as besides the ease he wore the same clothing as doctors and sometimes patients mistakenly referred to him a doctor. His Regret was that he did not get full retirement which comes after 20 to 30 years on the job. In preparation for coming back to Jamaica he returned to working as a porter and painter.

In Jamaica

My husband says that he was the one who decided to come home, but I was the one who always encouraged him to save some money and buy this little house. My husband's explanation for deciding to come home is he had gotten fed-up of England, it was too cold, and he did not have many friends there. On one of his trips to Jamaica he saw his old friends who encouraged returning. But since coming home these very same friends and relatives have become jealous because we can retire while they have to be still working. Jamaicans are very bad-mind. I remember once while living in England that I did not have a job because my foot was sick. I wrote and told my sister and her response was, "I wish if your foot did rotten off." My own relatives did not care about me—they wanted was the foreign money.

Life is very lonely in Jamaica for me too. My husband goes where he wants but I have to stay home to do house work, cook and wash. I said to my husband, "look I can find my own bread and butter, for I have my pension from England too. I am an independent woman, but you are my husband I expect you to take me out too." I have heard of the returned residents association but all these things take money and we did not get the big pension like other people. My husband did not start to work at the hospital until 10 years before coming home, and since we retired before age 65 had to wait for 10 years before receiving our pensions.

Sometimes I miss England for the amenities, the shopping and when I don't feel like cooking I could always have food delivered. If my husband were to die I would go live with my son in Canada. [Since this interview her husband died and she is now going to visit her son in Canada and plans to sell her house in Jamaica.] Life in Jamaica is too confining and I cannot go out by myself for the people in the community watch and peep, and Jamaica has become very dangerous. Take this little community, we have had 2 murders—last year a man was waiting for a taxi when a man in car drove up and asked if he knew another person and shot him dead. We went to the dead yard and have since received death threats on our telephone. We went to the police several times to find out who made the call but the police ran us around by telling us to come back.

Merissa's story also illustrates how wives viewed their return migration experiences. They expressed a preference for their lives abroad and their ability to escape the daily chores of cooking, washing clothes and making plans for their homes. Returnee wives were distraught and like Merissa complained, "he can go anywhere and spend long hours playing dominoes with friends." But these wives felt that it was not socially acceptable for them to go out alone in Jamaica as they would suffer community censorship. One explanation for their feelings is that, while abroad women gained personal mobility and independence from community censorship. It was from this perspective that women perceived return migration to Jamaica and were far less willing than men to characterize their experiences abroad in racial terms, or their return as perfect.

Often women like Merissa voiced their feelings of being socially incapacitated by being in Jamaica and consequentially picked out the good things about being abroad, but picked out the bad things about Jamaica. This was very obvious as Merissa owned a washing machine and had a house maid. What is of sociological importance here is that both men and women recast their experiences of return based on their economic independence and feelings of dependency in their marital relationships (Bennett 2002). Though women experienced racism abroad, they recast their experiences in light of their distance from family, goods, services, liberation from house chores and from dependency on male incomes. On returning to Jamaica, wives highlighted their need for strong family relations with their husbands through inclusion in social activities and emotional support. As Merissa said, "I can find my own bread and butter. I am an independent woman, but you are my husband. I expect you to feed me and I also expect you to take me out too."

The way wives spoke about their return was not unknown to husbands. While abroad some men in the sample even divorced their previous wives because they thought that they were not doing the things that would make return-ing possible. John and Harold also said that when their wives wanted to take trips abroad they used visiting their children as excuses.

Voluntary Returnees with High-Colonial Capital

The second pattern was found among high-colonial capital return migrants from England (illustrated by Cleveland's life story) and post-1965 voluntary returnees from America (illustrated by Hugh's life story). While abroad they accomplished educational and financial goals within 7 to 15 years, because they left Jamaica with the needed colonial capital to accomplish set goals over a short period of time, and their attitudes earned them respect even when faced with racism.

On returning, migrants within this category did not maintain foreign ac-cents, dress, walk, consumption habits, and ideals which would have made them odd to countrymen. As a consequence they did not have to negotiate re-entry into community life by buying groceries for the needy, giving away more money than countrymen asked for, and by making jokes with countrymen. Such mi-grants re-melded their footing in community life, in well paying jobs, and by conducting privately owned businesses.

Cleveland's Story

I was born in Kingston, Jamaica where my father was a tailor who owned his own establishment. My mother was a housewife. I have only 1 sister from the union, but my mother had 3 children from a previous relationship. My eld-est brother joined the RAF in the mid forties when the migration to England started. We lived in upper Oxford Street, across from Chitolah Park, for about a year and then moved to Kencott Road which was located in uptown Kingston. We moved probably because my parents felt it was better for raising children.

We lived at Kencott until my father left for England to do better. I can't remember the year, but about a year after my mother left to join him. He might have gotten fed up because his establishment was broken into several times.

He started out in London as a tailor, but felt he was not being paid for his expertise. He later moved on to work at Firestone Tire Factory and retired from this company. After my mother left, I went to live with my married half sister who was a cosmetologist. My full sister became a dressmaker. At age 11, I went to Excelsior High School, and graduated at 17 and took my first job as a store clerk.

Not many months later, I took a second store keeper position with another company which needed staff for their newly installed manufacturing process. At this time I still lived with my sister and was able to save enough money to purchase a motor car. Eventually, on my second job I became a supervisor, who also trained new employees, but in 1959 at age 25, I developed the urge to study engineering. This interest came from working with the new machines, and I wanted to get better qualifications and see what England was like. I had no ideas about England except from history books and what teachers said. To initiate migration I just told my father, he booked my passage and I left for London in 1959. I did not have any assets except for a car which I sold, but the purchaser cheated me by not completely paying for the car.

I went to England on the Camito Banana ship with 10 other passengers.

On arriving in South Hampton I took the train to London but did not see anybody I knew, and so took a taxi to my father home. My father thought I was coming on the boat train, that's how we missed each other. On the train I saw row and terrace homes, and brick buildings which were not in Jamaica. I was still a little apprehensive having not seen anybody at the station.

From the beginning, I did not intend to stay in England because I never wanted my children to grow up as second class citizens—I was a patriotic Jamaican. If I wanted to remain, then when British Passports were being issued in 1962, I would have taken one. I already had a good life in Jamaica, a supervisor's job, and my own motor car, but went to England to broaden my life experiences, and study Mechanical Engineering; a degree that was not offered in Jamaica at the time. All together I spent 7 years working and studying.

In England

At first I lived with my father and step-mother for 3 years. By now my mother had died and my father was remarried. My first room was in a bachelor's pad. After moving in I realized what a "bachelor's pad" meant. This was English euphemism for a homosexual den. I summarily moved out to live with some other Jamaicans, with whom I remained until returning to live in Jamaica.

Two weeks after landing in England I started looking for work. To find my first job, I took the advice from other Jamaican migrants and went to the "Labor Exchange." This was a government run unemployment agency which also distributed welfare to the unemployed. When I told the Labor Exchange personnel I was a store keeper and manufacturing supervisor in Jamaica it was like they did not hear me. They sent me to an ice cream factory, where there were lots of students, but I could not perform the job to fill lollipop bags. I told the manager and the next night he made me wash down lollypop molds, but that was too monotonous and required no mental abilities. My second and third jobs as a draughtsman were an improvement over the first job. As a draughtsman I had the opportunity to design the drawings for small appliances and other products.

I also applied to an English university in 1959 and was accepted to pursue a certificate program of study in mechanical engineering. Acceptance was based on meeting the matriculation requirements of a high school diploma. The whole program took 7 years of attending evening classes. The first 5 years covered the core engineering courses and the final 2 years rounded off my academic experience with elective courses like Business Administration. I can remember that at the end of the first year, my grades were so good that the school encouraged me to attend full time day classes, but I needed to also work and did not take up the offer. At the end of the program I was endorsed as a mechanical engineer and could have joined the Institute of Mechanical Engineers but didn't. Maybe I should have, but now it would be of little purpose since I am retired.

I did not join any associations in England, but knew that workmen's clubs existed to meet the recreational and networking needs of black persons with blue collar jobs. I did not join as nobody invited me. Instead I was part of an itinerant cricket team and also played dominoes for lunch money.

Before going to England, I had friends of different ethnicities and the issue of race did not enter my mind. The significance of race did not change in England, for middle class Jamaicans experienced little racism, but the lower class people experienced a lot because English society felt that the lower class Jamaicans came to take their jobs, and that class of Jamaicans could not read. Every bad experience though, that the lower class suffered was not simply about race; it was also that the lower class Jamaicans never learned to mix with people of other cultures from the time they were in Jamaica. Instead Jamaicans mixed with Jamaicans from all different classes.

The problem that poorer Jamaicans experienced in England came from a mixture of their inferior social class habits, culture and skin color. If one looked for race, then it was easily found, but the issues Jamaicans faced was more complex. Take an example from my third job, whenever the English employees went out together, I felt excluded. I then went to my boss and expressed my desire to leave because of being excluded. But to my surprise, my boss said I should not leave. Today I still correspond with some of my co-workers from this job over these forty years through Christmas cards. Even when I left England a coworker and his wife came to the wharf to say goodbye.

In 1965 at age thirty-two, I began planning my return to Jamaica. My first concern was finding a job through the Jamaican High Commission. Although the High Commission was staffed by Jamaicans, when I asked about jobs in Jamaica, they told him to write Kingston—I felt "brushed off." One day while reading an English newspaper I found an advertisement for a mechanical engineering position in Jamaica. I thought to myself, they may have tried to find a Jamaican to fill the position, as was their policy, but did not, and my applying in England would be a surprise.

My application was well received and I was interviewed for the position in England. I did not understand that I could have been hired as an expatriate. What this meant was I would have been paid in the equivalent English Pounds, and if I did not like the job on going to Jamaica, the parent company would be obligated to pay for my return trip to England.

I returned to Jamaica in 1966 with my only possession; a motor car which my father had bought me 2 years before coming home. I was not told by my recruiter that my new employer would pay for my travel back to Jamaica, or else I would not have paid my own way, and then I would have had more money to spend on my vacation before turning out for work. My job entitled me to housing, but no houses were available because the construction company that was building these new houses had shut down. I lived with the family of a teacher in Linstead (a rural area), to whom I was introduced by the father of a friend.

I was unaware of any changes in my personality brought about by living in England. But one night I remember having a punctured tire and two men who were playing dominoes paused to help me with changing the tire. While in conversation one remarked that I had an accent, or was putting on, as if from some other country. But I have never had anybody identify me as "odd" or "English. From the time of my return in 1966 I have seen many changes that current return migrants might find strange:

i) In 1966 I could walk the streets at night without fear. Now there are places I cannot go—even in the day time.

ii) People no longer are cordial by saying hello to each other. I can remember if an older person came on a public bus, I saw it as my duty to give that person my seat. Now, people push each other out of the way.

iii) Politics has changed because turfs have been created and protected by gunmen whom the politicians arm. This gun culture is further reinforced by the emergence of drugs and the dealers need to protect their profits and merchant-dise. Up to the 1970s Jamaican society was doing very well, then came Michael Manley and that's when things started going down hill—it has not stopped since. Even in the 1980s with the change of political party, life was too severely damaged to be recovered in a short time.

The People's National Party has been in power for 17 years and has developed a good public service program but crime and poverty has increased dramatically. The society has kept them in power because voters want to deny Seaga (former head of the opposition political party in Jamaica) a Syrian, access to the Prime Ministership. The Prime Minister Patterson has boasted publicly, that in a crowd he looks no different from countrymen. Recent return migrants who left in the 1950s come home to find that black countrymen have achieved increased political power, and access to foreign goods. Politicians maintain popularity among voters, but have neglected to uplift countrymen who by and large have achieved economic mobility and education, but still lack traditional middle class social graces. In fact politicians pander to the crass behavior of voters to maintain power.

Since returning, I can remember one potential negative situation when my English boss identified that the silicone in the boiler was too high and began to rant and rage at me. I said nothing but talked with him in his office. I told him, "you know I am not in charge and if you talk like that in the future to me, I will leave." The manager apologized and we became friends. In comparison another worker ranted and raged over a similar incident, and as consequence he soon left the job. When the manager became plant manager I followed in his foot step and became plant manager in later years.

Return migrants in the sample from the U.S. tended to have completed formal high school, and held professions in Jamaica, but they went abroad to complete set goals, return home and settle in jobs, and businesses. An excerpt from Hugh's life story is presented to illustrate the patterns in high-colonial capital returnees from the U.S.

Hugh's Story

I was born in Tabernacle, St. Ann, Jamaica on 17 of July, 1955. My father was a farmer and truck operator/businessman, and my mother operated a grocery shop and bar. I am the 11th child of 12 children. Growing up I walked 2 miles to school barefooted until Bata shoe store came in with Mr. Robin plastic shoes which cost about 5 shillings. Every Sunday we walked to Alexandria Methodist Church. My parents were not rich.

As a youngster we woke at 5:00 a.m. to milk the cows, (we used the milk for our breakfast), tie out the goats, and feed the pigs before going to school at 8:00 a.m. My father was very strict, and we had very little fun time to play cricket and marbles.

At age 15, I was saved by my bigger sister who took me to Kingston to attend a private high school. Though I was in Kingston, every holiday I came home to help my father work on his truck. I did so well at this new school in 3rd form that my teachers put me into 4th form—in the same year.

At age 16, I passed my first external examination called Jamaica School Certificate, and during the following months passed an additional 7 JSC subjects. Things started to change because my father then came and told me that I passed; this was unusual.

In 1973, I went into form 5 and passed 3 Ordinary Level subjects (Ordinary Levels is an external examination from England). August 1974 was another turning point in my life, when I went to the Jamaica School of Agriculture to pursue a Diploma teaching course in Agricultural Science. I made this career choice without any input from my parents, and I received a full government scholarship to complete this course.

After graduating I taught at Kempshill Secondary in Vere, Clarendon. At this point I got away from working on my father's truck. But because of the work ethic gained from home, at Kempshill Secondary I became the only teacher to produce enough food to satisfy the needs of the institution and also sell the school's extra farm products to the general public. Despite my success, I left because the principal continued to give me the same dull 3rd form students from year to year.

During my time at Kempshill, with the help of my father, I bought this gas station in September 1981. Things ran smoothly at the gas station for about 3 years, but then the underground storage gas tanks started to leak fuel and the gas company which owned the tanks would not refund the money for replacing the tank; so I stepped away from the business in 1985. I needed cash quickly and migrated to the U.S. in 1986 as my mother had filed for me.

In New York I attended York Community College, majoring in business administration and accounting. My aim was to gain education and capital for my business in Jamaica. I thought that since I was a teacher in Jamaica, I could probably find a teaching job there. But, then the reality set in, as in America I could not get a good job; they wanted to hire me as a para-professional. This was a rude awakening. I then took a job as a horticultural plant technician to water office plants. They paid me US$6 per hour and this was more than what the government was willing to pay. In 3 years I got 3 promotions to earn US$10 per hour.

I then took a job delivering coffee and water, and was in charge of vending machines. Under my supervision water distribution grew. I can remember how I earned the respect and business of customers by making prompt deliveries on the Westchester route. As a regular deliveryman I built the number of vending machine from 30 machines to 110 machines. Based on my efficient delivery in New York, my company received the franchise from Bank of America.

My company then bought another company and this was when I learned about racism. My company planned to send me to do refrigeration school, but when they brought in another man who was white they told me, "Hugh you know we have to send Anthony to do the refrigeration because the people cannot understand your accent." They also used my beard as an excuse. I told them to give me the route because nobody wanted to do it as we paid toll and gas from US$100 dollars each day. Also the company was always behind deliveries there. After knowing the route well, I brought the delivery of goods from 3 days to a same day deliver; as long as the order was called in before 7:00 a.m. When the rest of the hospital saw how well the system ran the whole hospital came to my company. I had a doctor on my route on Kimberly Avenue who told me that when I leave he would give the contract to another company.

I did this for about 2 years, then I started to repatriate by taking stuff little by little to Jamaica. I had planned to return to Jamaica in 5 years but stayed 9. As soon as the route became profitable the boss came back to me and said they had someone doing the vending. I willingly gave them back the Westchester route and I took back the vending and rebuilt it. During this period in 1990 I started working part-time at a barrel company picking up barrels in the evenings. They called me Speedy Gonzales because I knew where to find all barrels. Customers started requesting me. Eventually they started to give me choice routes. Once I went for a barrel at 6:00 a.m. but arrived at 5:00 a.m., the lady called her friends and I came back with 14 barrels and a bicycle. This work ethic came from my early discipline in Jamaica.

In December 1995 I came back to Jamaica because I had pushed enough hand carts in America and had only received salary twice in my life. I figured that I had enough money as by this time I had finished one of my gas station buildings and removed the old leaky gasoline storage tanks. I took back a lot of customer service experience from the U.S. as this is what is missing from businesses in Jamaica.

Some people saw me at first as a foreigner coming back home with American ideas about customer service and good work. My belief is that since rain, snow or hail does not stop the postman in America, so it should be here in Jamaica. As soon as the customer enters to door they should receive a Cave Valley Howdy-do, and shelves must be stocked at all times as nobody buys from an empty store.

The biggest problem now at the gas station is work ethic and getting people to work all day, and every day as they do in America. I am currently initiating a culture of accountability and good customer care in the school through teaching agriculture. We must deliver and be responsible. As long as the goods are not delivered it must be returned or money received for them. Every time I change work shift there is a balance sheet problem. For example, one lady came up JA$15,000 short and all she said was, "I don't know what happened." To curb this problem I have had police lecture my staff on accountability. Every 2 weeks we have lectures before opening. This has cut the loss down to manageable levels.

In Jamaica besides being a businessman I am Chairman of the local primary school board, and a Justice of the Peace. I take great pride in introducing the community to computer literacy. Currently I would like to implement a software program which caters to slow learners.

Very little, if anything, has changed in Jamaica over the years except the government. Crime has changed with the influx of cell phone technology and the wave of deportees. Crime was always there but has climbed since communication technology has improved. There is little or no crime in Cave Valley and we can still sleep with our doors open.

The problem with returnees is that they cannot afford the life abroad and in Jamaica. Very few returnees earned degrees abroad and so their income is relatively very small. Some returnees put their money on fixed deposit and others do foolishness with their money. Most returnees from the U.S. earn around US$300 per week in pension. The English come back and spend their money fast expecting more at the end, but there is usually no more. My cousin, for example, came back from England with JA$7,000,000 to build a house, and I told him that was not enough—but he went ahead anyway. Every night he went to karaoke with a different girl on his arm and now he owes me JA$500,000. He has little savings and now each month must wait on his pension. I helped him to finish the house with my own money, but in the end he told me that he did not owe me any money.

On returning to Jamaica, return migrants from America were relatively young, and avoided the historical faux pas associated with pensioned returnees from England of not holding jobs, and being too different. They made a decided effort to avoid being identified as ever having been away and were successful at camouflaging their identity as "Yankee" by not talking with an accent, and by participating in the community life like their countrymen.

When asked about their experience with racism in America all responded that they did not have many racial problems, mainly because the time that they spent in America was focused on accomplishing set educational goals, and they set out to avoid the well known racial inferior status by being the best at their jobs.

Fellow mid-colonial capital returnees who not only spent 30 to 40 years abroad to achieve pensions, but also earned educational credentials distanced themselves from members of their group who spent 30 or more years abroad to only earn pensions. Three examples stood out: Paul who was a mechanical engineer commented that his fully pensioned peers could not read and write and abroad they did not even open a bank account, choosing instead to save money under their mattress. A second returnee called Randall recalled that while abroad his peers mocked him for attending university. However, now he felt better adjusted than they were, from having returned early with a partial pension from England, a full pension in Jamaica, as well as ownership of his farm.

Interestingly Paul and Randall being more literate spearheaded the formation of returned associations to serve the interests of others from whom they distanced themselves.

Patterns Across Returnees' Perceptions

All mid-colonial capital voluntary return migrants who stayed away for 30 to 40 years complained about crime, the decay of discipline in Jamaican society which some said started under the Manley regime, and the abject poverty of countrymen who constantly solicited them for money. These returnees were also surprised by the despair among Jamaican youths and their expectation of dying at a young age. These expectations about non-longevity, returnees' claimed were adopted from violence portrayed in American movies and the experience of downwardly mobile African-Americans. Some Jamaican youth, returnees said, were willing to do anything to survive daily as to them tomorrow was not theirs. Fully pensioned mid-colonial returnees who spent 30 to 40 years abroad saw themselves as those who knew about real discipline and as agents of change who returned to make individual Jamaicans "better." This really meant that returnees wanted countrymen to adopt an industrious attitude which resulted in mimicry of returnees' mobility from poverty to wealth. It was not only that the homes belonging to returnees who had the most foreign pensions were luxurious but they desperately desired to set the pace for the transformation of Jamaican neighborhoods into luxury communities, where countrymen had a community spirit.

To help, some of the fully pensioned returnees from England offered to teach the skills which were useful to them in Britain, but to countrymen these skills were unwanted. One returnee from England said that he educated himself in England in the art of welding. On returning to Jamaica he tried to teach young men his trade by asking them to bring welding materials and he would provide the theory, but nobody responded. The returnee felt that other Jamaicans wanted easy money, but were unwilling to learn the very skills which enabled returnees to earn a living abroad. Even the relatives of returnees only wanted money. For Merissa, when she explained to her relative in Jamaica that her leg was sick and she could not send any money, the relative in Jamaica said, "I wish if your foot did rotten off."

Given the impoverished Jamaican economy, there may have been alternative reasons for the non-responsiveness of the young men. For example, the cost of welding materials could have been outside of the income of the average Jamaican who would benefit from learning a trade and in any case countrymen who could afford welding supplies would gravitate towards easier trades in established institutions. But, the returned resident in question took the response of Jamaicans to his teaching efforts to be symbolic of a general malaise among countrymen to work as the returned resident did abroad, and to reject what was good for them.

Mid-colonial capital returnees' with the most pensions in the sample reported that countrymen told them, "Nobody can come change Jamaica, go back where you came from." But these rejected pensioned return migrants, especially from England, still wanted to "feel like somebody" and persisted in giving gifts to Jamaican institutions and to countrymen who constantly asked them for money. However, the gifts were often received without gratitude and this did not satiate the needs of returnees to be identified as agents of change. For example, one returnee who was away for 30 years gave his female domestic helper a Christmas card and a Jamaican $1000 note, but she did not say thank you. In another case the Returned Residents Association made a gift to a local hospital but the hospital did not acknowledge the gift with the expected thank you.

When the expected cordiality was not extended, returnees distanced themselves physically and emotionally from Jamaican society and those from England closed ranks among Returned Residents Association members. Often returnees who had been away for many years questioned their return home and asked, "do I really belong back home among these Jamaicans?" Use of the words "these Jamaicans" drew the ire of countrymen.

Returnees expressed much fears about their identity as foreigners, the frequent news reports about high level financial institutional fraud, and incidences of robbery and murder of returnees. Some return residents said, "If we had visited before actually returning then we would not have come back."

Home security was an extremely important issue as returnees expressed little trust in the police force. Residents reminisced that abroad the police had to respond within a certain period of time. But not so in Jamaica where the police had turned up the next day or not at all stating that they did not have a car. Take the case of Merissa, she asked the police and telephone company to trace a life threatening telephone call, but to no avail. Even though the phone company was directed to do so by the police and the technology was available. The lack of law and order was so perverse that returned residents felt that the police wanted to be given money before responding to their case.

In Jamaica receipt of services from government offices and public business-es was not always an entitlement, but was often received through dense social networks where countrymen knew each other. This was true even where getting a land line telephone was concerned and one had the required money to pay connection fees. Herby and Angela from England related how they were told that there were no telephone lines available, but after meeting a countryman who had contacts in the local telephone company they had service by the following day. This was not the case in England where returnees felt protected by the po-lice and laws prohibiting kickbacks and deferential treatment.

Countrymen's Perceptions of Returnees

Since social identity results from what others say, I spoke with several countrymen about their perceptions of returnees, I here present the views of, a mayor, two high school teachers and a realtor from one town where return mi-grants, and especially those from England, live in high concentration, and the views of a primary school principal from another more rural town.

The Mayor

Returned residents and especially those from England have been a big boost to the parish's economy and we are grateful for their presence. Many of the new houses and businesses are owned by them and they bring pensions and needed foreign currency to keep other local businesses viable. The returned res-idents are special because we know that there are many migrants who would like to return but are unable to because they simply do not have the money.

In addition to cash, returned migrants have reminded Jamaicans what civil society is about—they form community associations which cleanup the neigh-borhoods, and make generous donations to Christmas funds and to local hospit-als.

Some say that returned residents have been exploited by residents through increased land and building costs, but it is a free market and the prices have simply grown from the increased demand for land, building supplies and ser-vices. It is not only returned residents who pay higher prices but all Jamaicans.

Both the principal and the mayor agreed that returnees from England brought a modicum of civility to Jamaican life, because in England they achieved middle class wealth and traces of Victorian English graces. The principal said:

A lot of returnees have moved into our community and have formed crime watch, and citizens associations. But Jamaicans do not appreciate them because the Jamaican society has become so indiscipline. I went to England and I was shocked to see how well behaved people are there—if you stand in one place too long, a line forms behind you, and this is what returnees from England bring back to Jamaica—discipline.

The perceptions of the two teachers Ann and Lewin concurred with the Mayor's:

A large percentage of those who return contribute in a positive way to the development of the country. Because of the weakness of the Jamaican currency, returnees are more financially stable than their counterparts who remain in North America and Europe. Returnees invest in real estate and establish businesses, and some are highly trained and skilled individuals whose expertise is usually in demand.

However, for Sharon, the realtor, some returnees could be "aggressive and know it all" persons who had lost their ethnic identity bonds (Wellman 1979), and Jamaicans merely in the color of their skin. Sharon argued that, by and large returnees who left Jamaica without the necessary social capital still lacked true middle class Jamaican status because of their blue collar professions abroad and poor use of the English language. Lewin listed the negative perceptions she held of return migrants:

> They can become social misfits.
> They can add to an already overpopulated area
> Their resettlement can be traumatic and re-acculturation can be terrifying
> They can take jobs from countrymen because of their skills.
> They can become targets for criminals.
> They can cause crime and violence to increase.

Other countrymen supported their poor perception of returnees by questioning the rationale for: multi-storied luxury homes perched high on precipitous cliffs when there was only a return migrant husband and wife; frequent trips abroad for medical care when the cost of traveling could purchase the best health care in Jamaica, and, freely loaning money based friendly verbal contracts. Lewin summed up the poor perception of pensioned returnees by stating that,

> Not all returnees are seen as the upper crust. Most of them return home to enjoy the sort of life style they could not enjoy in the Motherland. One must remember that a large percentage of those who went to England in the 1950s were migrants of humble means, and uneducated, etc.

DISCUSSION

The analysis strongly supports a conclusion that the predicament faced by voluntary return migrants was related to their colonial capital at the time of migration, and to subsequent shifts in their identity and mobility experienced abroad. High-colonial capital migrants who went abroad and completed university credentials experienced the best reception abroad and return migration reception from countrymen. This category of migrants also left Jamaica with enough colonial capital to earn the respect of others, and on returning dismantled accents, to avoid being identified as ever having lived abroad.

In contrast, the experiences of mid-colonial capital migrants who remained abroad to secure only full pensions, were far more complex as their financial mobility did not entirely improve their social status. Abroad, although they became financially stable, yet they were still black persons who were deficient in education and social graces. In Jamaica they maintained adopted foreign ways, built luxury homes, and were praised for fueling the Jamaican economy with needed foreign currency, and acts of civility. At times members of this group who went to school and worked abroad set themselves apart from pensioned return migrants who did not improve their colonial capital—except for earning foreign pensions.

Countrymen felt returnees with mid-colonial capital were still lower class social misfits with money and foreign accents; added to already overpopulated areas, threatened to the job security of countrymen; caused crime and violence to increase; and, contributed to inequality by building unnecessarily large luxury homes merely to establish their economic superiority over poorer Jamaicans. Even the civility of this category of returnee was quietly seen by countrymen as odd and out of sync with emerging shifts in Jamaican life.

The high regard that returnees who remained abroad to earn full pensions held about their financial gains was contravened by coterminous shifts in financial mobility among countrymen. These shifts forced returnees to compete with countrymen by building bigger luxury homes than the many large homes which were built by countrymen who had not migrated. Sometimes countrymen made fools of returnees by building their homes from the remittances returnees sent home to take care of loved ones or in preparation for returning. In a sense, the deference countrymen gave in times past to returnees no longer existed, as countrymen, and not just the lucky or gifted, aspired to higher standards of living and knew about the menial jobs some returnees did abroad.

The negative effects of return migration were not unitary but had differential gender effects. Male and female returnees who remained abroad to earn full pensions recast their return experiences in light of the perceived freedoms which their labor force participation abroad gave them. Wives perceived they had not only returned to the warm climate of sweet Jamaica, but to colonial prejudices, and the drudgery of housework. Consequently, among couples this gender effect helped to drive the repeated cycles of their migration and return, as periodically spouses went abroad not only for medical care, or to break the monotony of being with countrymen but to relive freedoms, and then return to sweet Jamaica.

Faced with these cross cutting challenges, fully pensioned mid-colonial capital returnees lived liminaly. They felt like true Jamaicans but would not encourage return migration. They felt that Jamaica was sweet in climate but they were more comfortable abroad where civility made social life more predictable than Jamaica, where they were constantly solicited for money and targeted for crimes by their own relatives. In reaction, pensioned mid-colonial capital returnees constructed thick social fields among themselves which negated their negotiation of full re-entry with countrymen and family. In the case of mid-colonial capital return migrants from England, they resorted to the same strategies of closing rank among themselves as they employed in England. Those pensioned retired returnees who could afford to, also maintained condominiums abroad—this enabled them to associate with enclaves of equally discontented Jamaicans, away from Jamaica.

At least for two returnees skin color was significant. Reg married a brown skinned woman and felt that his experiences in life would have been improved if he were only light skinned. Cleveland married a lady from the Netherlands because he felt that no Jamaican woman would be as good to him as she was.

This research adds to return migration literature by identifying how colonial capital at the time of migration affects two categories of voluntary return migrants, and how coterminous shifts in mobility and identity among returnees and countrymen make their lives unhappy. Although fully pensioned mid-colonial capital returnees avoided the mistake of those return migrants who had come home within 5 years during the 1950s, only to find that they did not have enough money to overcome social prejudices, yet the changes in Jamaica, and prejudices about colonial capital offset the status of their long years spent earning pensions. In addition both interviewed countrymen and returnees used prejudice about each other's colonial capital to temper the other's mobility.

CHAPTER THREE
You look Like a Fool Returning with Nothing:
Involuntary Return Migrants

Standing in the Montego Bay airport customs line, I saw young men walking single file in an enclosed hallway. Some were dressed casually but others wore blue coveralls. They were deportees who had traveled on a regular Air Jamaica flight in the economy class seating section of the airplane. Apparently there is no standard operating procedure, as some interviewed deportees claimed they arrived home unescorted, while others reported that they were accompanied by U.S. Air Marshals who quietly ushered them through Jamaican customs and placed them in holding cells. Later the Jamaica police took them to local police stations. Yet other deportees reported that they were released without much questioning, and others said they answered questions about whether they had any family in Jamaica. These questioned deportees remained locked up until someone identified them. After positive identification, deportees said they were finger printed, released, and warned that if they committed any crimes the police would be in hot pursuit.

Migrants who are deported have lost their legal right to even visit the country from which they are deported, but may still travel to other countries. Deportees who were interviewed did not have the funds or interest in pursuing international travel—Jamaica was their iron cage in which lived without thought of escaping to achieve financial mobility abroad. This downward shift had serious backlash implications for their lives in Jamaica, as all return migrants are expected, at the very least, to have increased the financial element in their colonial capital.

This chapter exposes some of the major life altering circumstances which brought about deportees' demise, and evaluates how low-colonial capital at the time of migration and associated downward shifts in identity, and mobility affects their return migration experiences.

What altered migrants' dreams of achieving wealth abroad and incurred their deportation? When interviewed deportees migrated abroad, they expected to realize long entrenched hopes and dreams of achieving wealth. Unfortunately, they were naive about the social and economic outcomes of natives and immigrants who shared their phenotype and lived in impoverished inner city with single parents.

Existing sociological literature consistently argues that, post-1965 immigrant children who are both, of African ancestry and live in impoverished inner cities must cross a narrow bottle neck to occupations requiring advanced training. Post-1965 immigrant parents can assist their children to cross the narrow bottleneck by expending various forms of capital on their academic preparation. Usually insufficient financial capital is accumulated while living abroad (Portes et al. 1993), thus the economic class migrants occupy in their home societies, and the various capitals parents take abroad are extremely important variables which determine the outcome of their children abroad.

The parents of interviewed Jamaican deportees arrived abroad with little colonial capital and especially the element of expendable capital. Often they made the sacrifice of leaving their spouses and children behind. Over the course of several years, families were reunited as parents accumulated the necessary financial capital and successfully demonstrated to immigration officials that they were able to care for left behind spouses and children in the host societies. However, once children arrived in the US and England, the resources of families who occupied the lower socio-economic strata proved insufficient to meet personal needs much less assist children to cross the narrow bottleneck in opportunities.

The literature attributes the continued impoverishment of lower socio-economic immigrants abroad to their stigmatized identity as social inferiors (Waters 1999) and to their lack of well established networks which provide valued resources. Single female Jamaican parents of deportees provide an illustrative example of how the absence of networks was disadvantageous. Their achieved financial stability was based on working long hours in multiple jobs, and since they lacked the support of extended families to provide child care, their ability to meet necessary child development needs was attenuated. In the absence of vigilant parental supervision, the influence of peer pressure gained ground, and 1.5 generation children were in some instances introduced to the use and sale of crack cocaine. Below are representative life stories which clarify how a concatenation of factors shaped the lives of low-colonial capital migrants who later became deportees.

Mark's Story

I was born in the parish of Manchester [a rural area of Jamaica] on the 3rd April 1967. I was born in my grandaunt's house where my parents lived. This was a little district called Chudleigh Path. I was one of 6 sisters and 1 brother. I was the 5th child. My daddy worked at the local bauxite company as a mechanic and my mother was a domestic worker. From my grandaunt's house my father bought some land in Porous and built a 2 room house for himself. From Porus we moved to Bellfield because the noise from living on the road side was too much and the house was bigger with 6 rooms.

In 1979 my mother's cousins helped her to get a 5 year domestic work visa to Queens, New York. When the visa expired she overstayed her time and went off to live with a relative who abused her and threatened to call the immigration. This made her work in the relative house for nothing. After a while she ran away from New York to other relatives in Chicago until she received her legitimate Green Card.

All this time my father remained in Jamaica working at the bauxite mine. He struggled to take care of all 8 children—my older sisters were in high school and I was in primary school. My mother was an illegal immigrant and could not send much money. Periodically she wrote, but her education did not permit clear communication, and Daddy could hardly understand her letters.

In 1984 my father happily quit his job at the bauxite mines and he along with 4 of my sisters migrated to New York. Two of my sisters did not finish high school, but they had to go because their coveted travel visas had arrived. Since the older sisters were the ones who migrated, life in Jamaica became difficult to manage because the brothers had to take care of the 2 younger sisters. Sometimes we went to my grandaunt for food, and periodically my mother sent money but my brother was not a good finance minister. It appeared that my father did not find a good job in the U.S. and was struggling financially. My mother also sent barrels of clothing, and food items around Christmas. The smell of the barrel was enough to me feel like I was abroad. When friends saw me with the clothes they said, "barrel come."

The following 2 years my mother took up the remaining 4 children. I was happy to go. The day that I went to the U.S. Embassy I remember clearly that the immigration officer looked at me and said "I hope you are not going to sell drugs." This statement gave me a good idea; in the back of my head I thought that may be a viable alternative.

My eldest sister came to Jamaica for us with the necessary documents. We arrived on the 6th of June 1986 in New York. It was a warm day and my mother's friend named Neville came to pick us up. After clearing U.S. customs I saw my other 2 sisters. My first impression of America was, "this is the Big Apple; a golden dream come true." From the airport we drove to Brooklyn. Two of my sisters came to meet us. At the time they lived on Easter Parkway in a 6 story building with an elevator. All this was exciting as I never saw such a tall building before, or rode on an elevator. Neither had I seen the large roadways, fancy cars, and subway.

In the first week my siblings took me around New York, and showed a good time. Friends had welcoming parties, but by the second week their faces changed. Mama said with a long face, "you need to start going to school, find a part-time job because the winter is coming up and you would need a winter jacket." This was surprising as I did not think she would have told me this. I thought life would be a bed of roses and I did not think about working because in Jamaica children did not have to work.

The next day I applied to a trade center, but I did not have any clear cut ideas about what I wanted to be. Growing up I played with my father's tools and so applied to be a mechanic. My third sister took me to her job downtown at Jack's Bargain Center in Brooklyn where her boss paid me U.S. $50 per week to put out televisions on the sidewalk for display. Unfortunately, this job lasted for 2 weeks—riding on the subway cost US$2 per day and lunch cost about US$4.00 per day. On pay day I gave mama US$20, but she said, "this can't work, you need to find another job."

I obeyed and found another job in the newspaper as a mechanic at King Bear Mechanic Shop. They fixed front ends on motor cars, but I found out that they resold old parts to their customers. The labor was performed by a Haitian worker who appeared to me to be like a slave. Probably he did not even have a green card and so was willing to sand old car parts to make them appear new — all without the necessary preventative mask. After 1 week other workers found out that I knew about their car parts scam and they made up false allegations— the white boss said I was too slow, and another worker from Barbados alleged that I stole his tool. The boss then fired me and said if I told anyone about their car parts scam he would burn down my house and kill me and my family. I left crying and they did not pay me so I was penniless.

My 3rd job making mattresses in Queens, at Arise Futon Flow Company, was provided by a work agency. I did not know Queens was so cold. I bought size 13 shoes, although I really wore size 9, so that I could wear 4 thick socks to keep my feet from freezing. I felt the cold when I walked from my house to the subway and from the subway to the factory. This job lasted for 1 month— the boss was a Jew and started to fire all black men after we asked for a raise of pay; he appeared to dislike blacks. From my pay of US$160 per week I gave Mama $60 and kept the rest. I could balance my way now but this was not enough. In addition I received a US$10,000 school grant to buy tools and pay tuition.

Things were looking up when tragedy struck. Unfortunately, one night thieves broke into my Jamaican friend's car and stole the radio and my mechanic tools. These tools were bought from the student loan that I got from Burke's Trade Center. This was a turning point for I could not replace the costly tools. I made up my mind that I had to go do something else. The owner of the car from which my tools were stolen had gone to Texas as he usually did, to sell drugs. After each trip he looked real expensive, had on gold and was glittering. He even gave me a US$100 even though I was using his car. I told my friend that I wanted to come where he was to make some money. My friend said, yes, I could make good money without having to work so hard. About 1 week later he bought my plane ticket for Texas. I told my parents about going to Texas but they said, "don't go." My mother said, "it's drugs you are going to sell", but I said "no", all the time knowing they were telling the truth. I saw the strain my parents suffered and I wanted a way out.

I landed in Texas in about September and lived in a house called a "trap." This is a house from which drugs is sold. My trap was a furnished apartment in a 2 story house. My friend paid the rent. Our drug selling lasted for about 3 weeks. I sold drugs to an undercover drug enforcement agent, and the Dallas Police accused us of killing someone. They arrested us, took our finger prints and released us. I returned to selling drugs, until someone informed me that a warrant was out for my arrest. I thought that the warrant was for a traffic offense, but one evening I found out it was really a Federal warrant. I was on my way to deliver some crack cocaine but was pulled over by a police man. He took me of out the car and made me sit on the side walk with my hand over my head. I was wondering what I had done for him to do this to me. However, when I looked around many more police cars appeared and they had guns aimed at me. One police handcuffed me, placed his knee in my back and then lifted me by my feet and cuffs into the police car. From there I went to the county jail for 9 months and then spent 5 years in a federal penitentiary. My court appointed lawyers told me to plead guilty. I tried to hire a lawyer but he wanted US$30,000 and I did not have this amount. I pleaded guilty and received an 8 year sentence.

I went to school in jail but did not get my GED. I fought constantly with Mexicans who would squabble over the phone. Mexicans always wanted to use the phone and would knock on the windows. I also fought with whites over the television stations. After serving my sentence I was deported to Jamaica from the U.S. on November 19, 1993, and came to live in my parent's old home.

In the absence of a husband (Mark's mother was divorced from his father); Mark's mother looked to her children for economic support. Mark said that he had one pair of shoes which hurt his feet because they shrunk in the cold weather. At the end of a pay period he did not have enough money to replace these shoes and to also help his mother with the household expenses. This additional pressure to fill the economic void left by his father pushed him to seek for resolution in earning quick money by selling drugs—this activity eventually led to his deportation.

A second representative life story from James shares a common thread of experience with Mark's life of, leaving rural Jamaica during adolescence to live in an impoverished section of inner city of New York with a divorced mother. However, James's life story emphasizes the irreversible psychotic effects from drug use which can accompany 1.5 generation adolescents' downward economic mobility.

James's Story

I was born in a district called "Picky Picky" in Manchester Jamaica, and migrated at the age of 14 to join my parents in New York City. Although I have 2 brothers and 2 sisters, I am the oldest and only child for mother and father. One sister lives abroad and is in the U.S. Navy. My other sister lives in Jamaica and I know very little about her because she avoids me by not giving me much information about herself. One of my brothers died abroad.

Before leaving Jamaica I was a well disciplined, church going youth who clung to my mother. In New York things changed, I stopped listening to my mother and took up with friends. Mama couldn't show me anything. As soon as my parents said anything, I slammed the door in their face.

As the first child I expected to achieve a whole lot abroad, but went down the negative path. I feel that if I had lived among other positive influences in America then my end would be different. In upstate New York some blacks and whites get along this was shocking to me at first. I learnt over time that blacks should stick with other blacks as not all whites liked blacks. From the expression on the faces of possible white employers I understood not to apply for work there.

I migrated with the hope of participating in the good experience of going to college to become a computer technologist. But, I went to high school for only 2 years when trouble started. My parents told me to keep away from bad company with fellow Jamaicans and African Americans, but I continuously cut school and my grades fell. The final incident leading to being kicked out of high school occurred at about age 16 when I took a knife used to butter bread to school. I explained to the teacher after being caught with the knife that I forgot that I had the knife on me because my pants were baggy, like other American kids in my neighborhood wore. But he wasn't hearing all of that. After the expulsion I spent a lot more time on the streets and started to sell drugs.

My parents got me back into GED programs but friends laced my marijuana with a cocaine-angel dust concoction, which made me crazy. I was put in an institution for 10 months and took psychotropic drugs. I worked on my GED while in psychiatric care but did not complete program. I kept telling the teachers that I was scared of the gang influence in the hospital.

After being released from the psychiatric unit I witnessed a murder and was on witness protection moving from place to place—eventually to be charged with possession of drugs. While in U.S. prison, I noticed how blacks operated and started to study more. In this sense prison was a positive influence. The brothers in jail provided encouragement amidst the negative environment. Jail had the best lawyers and educators locked up.

Despite the protestation of parents, James maintained his association with other disobedient friends from Jamaica and native born African Americans. Unknown to James his friends laced his marijuana cigarette with a cocaine concoction which triggered his first psychotic episode. This incident led to a host of collateral damage as he was now a user and seller of marijuana and cocaine—for which he was arrested and deported.

The experiences Mark and James had with their mothers are not to be unexpected (Stinson 1991; Wallerstein et al. 1989). After a divorce, when one spouse is absent, the custodial parent often seeks for assistance from adolescent children (Weiss 1979) who like Mark and James can also take on new roles—as adults who were empowered to earn the desired economic support through any means possible —even the sale of drugs.

Neville, made an interesting comparison case as he migrated to the U.S. during his late twenties, after holding a job in Jamaica, and worked for 20 years in the U.S. before being deported. In the previous two cases Mark and James were free in the U.S. for only short periods of time, and did not hold long term jobs. The most pointed difference in Neville's life story is that he attributed his deportation to his adolescent need for attention which started in Jamaica.

Neville's Story
I was born in Chudleigh Manchester in 1952. My father worked at Alcan Jamaica Limited, Kirkvine Works as a storekeeper. He was the best in the business. My mother was a housewife and a seamstress. My sister did not wear one dress twice to a dance. I was the 3rd of 7 children. Life in Jamaica was rough as my father drank too much and there wasn't enough money. I got a government scholarship in 1963, but after about 2 years of going to high school I lost the scholarship because of poor performance. At night I had to watch for my father who would come in drunk and just thump me down for nothing. My sister could lock herself in her room to study, but we could not. This is the same house that I am standing in that this occurred. With the loss of the scholarship my mother now had to now pay for my education. This was when I started giving trouble. If they said wear black socks I wore white. I lost interest and did not want to go to school as everybody else wore long pants I was stuck in short pants and underwear that were too small.

My elder brother went to 3 schools and I did not, my parents would not give me a chance. I was very lonely and loneliness continued to plague my life abroad. To find solace I drank and acquiesced to peer pressure to use drugs. America was a zoo, but although I did not do drugs in Jamaica, the "zoo stuff" may have started there and only deepened in America. In Jamaica, I suffered many difficulties and felt disgruntled with the system of law. For one, while working as a policeman, my supervisor on the police force raped a woman in my presence. In addition, the woman to whom I was engaged was propositioned by my brother; this experience was very vexing. When my papers came for migration it was a welcomed relief to leave Jamaica and reunite with my mother and father in Fort Lauderdale.

Although I was mulatto, I identified with Jamaicans of African hue. But in America, I was frequently identified socially as part of white society and so heard the confidential jokes whites made about fellow Jamaicans who were of African hue. I remember drinking in a bar where one customer made disparaging remarks about Jamaicans being thieves and drug smugglers. In response, as the offending customer approached me, I slugged him.

But, migration did not fill my emotional void of loneliness. To gain the acceptance of peers and overcome deeper bouts of loneliness, I used drugs and drank alcohol. Life in the U.S. was a mere survival, as my income was never enough, and on my jobs as an aircraft gasoline supplier and as a building electrician faced the stigma of being Jamaican and inferior although I looked white in color. Even in instances where I taught others the job I was still classified as a second class citizen in America.

In the U.S., I lost everything; even my spleen. Whenever I use the bathroom I bleed, and as a consequence do not have the energy to even cut my own grass as I should. My vehicular negligence also claimed the life of my friend, and this accident was the reason for my deportation. However, I do miss the availability of jobs in the U.S.

Not all deportees were like James, Mark and Neville who willingly accepted their status of being deportees. The life stories of return migrants from England reflected this characteristic; they would not confess to their deportation. However, it was clear to informants, and countrymen that they had run amuck of the law in foreign countries. In the first of these two cases, Jay went to England on the invitation of his sister who intended to introduce him to the hardships of living abroad. Her intentions were not for him to stay, but Jay saw this as his chance to earn some money. After all he had come to England and so should not go back without the trappings of wealth to satiate the expectations his local community had of return migrants. To circumvent the visitor visa Jay enrolled in a community college program and after six months attempted to find work.

In the second case Bobby migrated to England as a visitor, but started his own business after 4 weeks and was married within 3 months. For Bobby, during these years it was possible for visitors to remain past their legally allotted time, as illegal immigration was not of paramount importance to English police. It was not until the arrival of "Yardy" gangs from Kingston that Jamaicans gained high negative social profiles in English society. Over the course of 9 years Bobby acquired much material wealth, enough to purchase a JA$7.5 million home in his local community and deal in expensive Jaguar cars; all while being a clothing designer and manufacturer. For those return migrants who knew

Bobby in London, his businesses were mere disguises for dealing in illegal drugs such as marijuana and cocaine.

When asked about his experience with racism in England, Bobby said that the system did not fight against him, but gave him opportunity to own valued resources that only the rich had in Jamaica. He did not see English whites as having better houses than Jamaicans; but the reverse. For example, he had 5 Jaguar motor cars at one time. Ultimately, Bobby felt that his own Jamaicans gave more problems than whites as they were the ones who robbed him in London at gun point.

Not all deportees were in their good senses or male's who committed crimes abroad. Some were female, but like male deportees they were 1.5 generation immigrants who suffered from poor family relations. The following case of Olivive supports this notion:

Olivive's Story

I was born on November 17, 1955 in the Montego Bay General Hospital. When I was about age 3 my parents bought land and built a shop in Kingston at White Hall Terrace off Red Hills Road. My mother was a floor sales clerk in Kingston and my father was a tile maker at Crichton Brothers. We rented out part of our shop and did a patty and cocoa bread business for 1 year in the other part of the building. There were 5 children from the immediate marriage and 2 outside. I was the first child from the union.

I went to Half Way Tree Primary School and Papine Junior High. The same went for the rest of the family.

I don't know where in the U.S. my father went, but he left when I was age 9 —in about 1964. My mother then migrated leaving us with the household helper and my grandmother who came from Montego Bay to visit. I heard that the helper was committed to us because she suffered from polio and had no family. She taught us Math, English, and good manners, and reinforced the good qualities that my parents started. My parents were good providers and sent money every Thursday without fail. Sometimes the helper sent me to change the currency. Our rent was paid from a different source, other than the money my parents sent but food money came out of the weekly mail.

My parents were gone for 4 years before they received our visas. After 2 years they might have visited us in Jamaica. All the children went abroad in March of 1972, but not me. I had an accident with a passenger bus belonging to the Jamaica Omnibus Service, and was on the orthopedic ward at University of the West Indies Hospital. The helper still took care of me and my father came to Jamaica with an extension for my visa. I was happy to be going abroad as I looked forward to the new things that could happen in my life. On arrival in the U.S. I planned to become an airline stewardess which would fund my way through medical school.

My father came to meet me at the airport since my mother was at work. She was a nursing assistant in nursing homes. After that job she got a job in a hospital which is what raised us. From the airport I saw tall trees, and smooth roads; not that I did not have smooth roads in Kingston. I was surprised to see the small lawns and how close the houses were to the streets. In other respects it resembled Kingston. My parents lived in the city of Washington, DC itself. The new home was large and nice and my siblings were there waiting along with the rest of the neighborhood. The house had 3 stories and a basement with a little window. All this was new as in Jamaica I never lived in a house as this. The bedrooms were small; I thought so. The verandahs in DC houses were different; they were not as low as ours in Jamaica and Americans called verandahs porches.

In 1972 I started high school in the 10th grade. I earned an A average over that 1st year and fitted in school okay—I was bright, and always a reader who was very knowledgeable. Additionally half of the things I did in the 10th grade I had already done in Jamaica.

In my neighborhood for the 1st year I did not associate with any Jamaicans. The neighborhood was made up of African Americans who were militant about their black power. The neighborhood had a few whites. The yards were well manicured, and dogs had to be fenced in. Their social outlook was upper middle class, doctors and teachers.

In the 11th grade I had an F. In my second year of puberty I started getting low self esteem. I fell short in classes and only worried about getting money and a job. I got a job in the Washington Youth Core Program and did baby sitting jobs. I also had a 2 year scholarship of $500 from the Woodridge Foundation to help replace my teeth with dentures and help with school expenses. In September 1973 I applied for a Student Work Study Program to work in the school. In the summer I worked in the recreational centers in the elementary school—this was like a summer youth camp.

I then decided to stop attending day classes because of money. For the first year Woodridge Foundation gave financial help from January to April and that summer I worked in a study program. As a policy students could not get the work study program for 1 year. Every year I kept other summer jobs, but the money was small. I tried going to night school but got kicked out because this young man tried to pick me up and I kissed my teeth. The boy reported me and the head person came and threw me out. He ruined my life. I did not graduate from high school. I had a lame leg from the bus accident which would swell up from an ulcer on the leg. I could not do anything without the high school diploma and my parents said nothing.

The year 1973 was memorable, as I went to my first all night Jamaican party with a Jamaican girlfriend. We went over to some guy's house that attended Howard University. Nothing happened sexually, but we just crashed from being tired. This was Washington, DC in the 1970s they took nothing from anyone. I was used to attending adult parties in Jamaica and stayed out until 4:00 or 5:00 a.m.

On the first night out, my mother told my siblings to lock the doors, so I had to wait until 7:00 a.m. when she came home. My girlfriend's mother called my mother to get clemency and my mother said okay. To avoid getting a beating I just went in got my stuff and went to live with my Jamaican girlfriend for a little while but I ended up staying from September to October. If my mother said anything I would move out to my girlfriend and her mother's house. If my girlfriend's mother said anything I would go home to my mother's house. My father never lived with us from the time we went to the U.S. This was unusual as this was the same father who would go to meet his wife although she just worked around the corner; he took his children to church, and looked after his children. I don't know what happened. I heard that he and my mother had an argument and he hit her. My daddy claimed that there were too many women in the house and he wasn't going to live with so many women—but he still visited or called. He came over in the day time especially if my mother complained to him about our actions.

My sister's school attendance was good until their first year in junior high school when attendance trickled to nothing. Only my brother continued his education on an athletic scholarship to a community college in California. He acquired a bachelor's degree in engineering, got married and returned home to Washington, DC with six children. The four girls became totally distracted from any academic work and did not graduate from any schools.

I was introduced to smoking weed by a Panamanian fellow and my girlfriend in 1975. My Jamaican girlfriend met this guy who introduced me to his friend. My girlfriend took a smoke every now and again and I took a smoke too. I started smoking herb but I did not do pills. I was part of a hippie black culture that emphasized black was for blacks, and black was beautiful. Black students would use their student loans to take trips to Africa. We went to parties every weekend—one week it was Jamaican, the next would be American, then Panamanian, and then Trinidadian. We were integrated ethnically in our social life.

It was a good thing because now blacks hold good jobs because we picked out the good made known that we wanted, and fought for our justice. We were tireless in what we wanted—we adopted the African culture in dress, recognized African Liberation Day, Malcolm X, and Martin Luther King's birthdays and we even dressed up to attend the Apollo Theater. Anything to big up blacks we pursued. We were proud of Washington, DC being 95% black— back then whites lived in Virginia. We also stood guard at Howard University to ensure that students completed their work. For example, if a student was using the main frame we would block the doors to make sure that student completed his work.

In 1979 I left home and hitch hiked for one month to visit my brother in California, and start a new life. Well one morning I went job hunting and scratched my brother's car, he threw me out and told me to return home because California wasn't a good place for me. The California pace was too fast, so I returned to DC and spent the winter hanging out with tractor trailer drivers. In route home to Washington DC, I was taken to truck stops in New York, Virginia, and Maryland. I started just traveling with truckers for fun and adventure, but at the end of every year I would go to California. First year I traveled central states and returned southern; the next year I went southern and returned northern.

In 1983 I decided to stay home and pursue my goal to attend DC University. But mom called the cops who sternly told me that I was of age and would be locked up if I returned. I told the cops that I had nowhere to go, so they took me to a shelter and dropped me off.

I moved from shelter to shelter in DC until I hitch hiked to Hartford, Connecticut. I had no place to live, and after 7 days the police took me to the Salvation Army in downtown Hartford. I made big strides by going back to high school to earn my GED. Then I got my nurses aid certificate to work in nursing homes because they had stopped using the Red Cross certificates. Welfare helped me to get an apartment but I mostly stayed at the YMCA, where I had access to a television and my own bathroom. This was in 1986 when Reaganomics permitted some people to go back to school. I started attending Community College and did general studies in liberal arts to get me up to snuff academically. Then I got a job with the government as a processing clerk in the state library which lasted for only 2 years because economic recession caused cut backs. After, I got a temporary job with the State Troopers with the possibility of getting a permanent position. The Troopers did a background check and the police who later came to arrest me said as soon as he punched in my name, the computer went wild. The Social Services had put out a warrant over the past 4 years claiming that I had defrauded them. I knew who had done this. There was a clerk who felt that I was too smart to be on welfare. I was arrested, charged and bailed all in three hours and lost the newly acquired job as a receptionist for the Connecticut State Troopers.

I then decided to finish my degree and learn something about computers from a certificate program that taught IBM software. It was during this tenure that I became caught up in the real drug/hard drugs (crack-cocaine) I started smoking to ease some pressure. I became lethargic and actually fell asleep in every class. I attended classes three twice per week from 10:00 a.m. to 7:30 p.m. This left me with three days to study and play. As the case was, I was now an amputee i.e. I had lost my leg in 1992 while I was working at the state library. Anyhow, I was on my way to acquiring an associate degree and that was good enough for me, but I fell along the way. I decided to visit my family in Toronto by trying to hike across the border, but I was stopped and sent to the nearest town. I resided there for three years when someone introduced me to some young drug dealers who lived next door; they asked me to be their middle person. At first I said no, but then accepted. I was arrested and charged with possession, trafficking, and sale of narcotics and sentenced to one to three years in prison, I did five months in jail and six months in maximum security because of my disability and there was only one prison which had a facility for the handicapped. It took them one year to deport me because I had written to the United Nations, and the Jamaican Consulate in New York, and had applied for a review of my case. The Jamaican Consulate' wrote back that I had no morals, and they could not do anything for me.

In Jamaica

After being in the U.S. for twenty-eight years I was deported. On arrival at the immigration office at the Montego Bay airport I was interviewed and released. "You are on your own" the officer told me, "you are free to go." That was good, as I was free—I hate being locked up. I walked out of the airport and asked the first Jamaica Union of Taxi Association (JUTA) driver if he knew where I could find a cheap room to rent. I had some money as after I got locked-up continued receiving my allowance until I began my sentence at the state prison. All of my accouchements that I had acquired between 1995 and 1998 were left behind except for the Alien Registration Card which was in the police custody—which they informed me I could send for after 5 years. I walked out of the airport in Montego Bay and a JUTA driver helped me to find a room on Church Street in Montego Bay.

From there I began my life as a return resident with US$150 on hand and US$800 in my U.S. bank account. Later I wrote my bank, and they sent me my money pronto.

Here I was in 2001, age 46, returning to Jamaica without any formal education or certificate, I had turned down so many short term certificates that could be of much use to my decorum and my country—now I had returned without anything. Everything was sucked out, but I had no intention of giving up. Jamaicans were not the losing type, it' a joke that we all had 200 jobs in the U.S. I put on my thinking cap and started a bank account which to my surprise became a scream—I had to be recommended by someone, just to open an account, and on the form I had to disclose the amount being lodged. Also my US$800 bank check was going to take 45 days to clear. I had to open with someone else meaning my account was really in somebody else's name, and I was the second recipient. I had asked my landlord to be one reference, but I needed two, so he sent me to a Justice of the Peace who helped by lodging my check to his account and giving me the money from his funds so I could pay rent and eat.

After a few weeks a young woman offered me a job in her gift and accessories shop. I worked for her for three years until September, 2004 when she decided that she could not afford to pay a two year retroactive increase in minimum wage, and that she was now powerful enough to meet out physical abuse. I took her to the department of labor but the judge said that because the young woman had given me her old clothing, she and I did not have an employee-employer relationship.

Now I was in the streets again because I could not pay my rent. I asked a male associate of mine to put me up but within 3 nights he threw me out. After trying to locate family here in Mobay, I found out my grandmother had died, and my uncle, the only living relative in Jamaica, could not put me up.

The code of the street was, deportees were fresh catch for every wrong doer in town. They would all be your buddy if you wanted to spread your wings in crime. Not me! I had always been a law abiding citizen and planned to remain so, even if I am a drug addict, which I am not. As a returning proud citizen, this country of mine has gone backwards.

After the friend threw me out, two days later I went to the Parish Council. This was my second visit, because at the time of the check cashing business, I had reason to seek shelter, but the Parish Council refused because I had money. But, this time I had no money or anything so after interviewing me, I was sent with a letter to the coordinator to allow me to stay until I could help myself. I was informed that the shelter was not the kind of place I would expect. Well, my expectation was not the issue, after walking the streets for two nights, I found myself surrounded by male predators who tried to get what they wanted; and that was sex. I was cornered by two unknown men while standing at an intersection but was saved by an acquaintance—he saw the danger and stopped. After explaining my dilemma, he told me to return to a nearby bar and wait for him as he was going to rent a room for me/us. But, he took me to his home for the rest of the night—which was all of three hours—he lived far, it was late, and I had to be out before his landlord's early rise at 5:30 a.m. So by 6:00 a.m. on January 3, 2005, I was walking down Barnett Street with JA$150.00 for breakfast.

I waited until 8:30 a.m. to go to the Poor Relief Municipal building which was on Union Street in Montego Bay. I explained my dilemma to a social worker who took my demographics and told me to wait to see the shelter director. After an interviewing conference, the shelter director decided to allow me to enter the Refuge of Hope Montego Bay Shelter for the Homeless. With a written letter of introduction and approval, I found my way to the shelter's location in a robot taxi with a driver who knew its direct location. It was open because it was after 5:00 p.m. and the desk was situated at the entrance. I handed the male attendant my letter, which he read, introduced myself and he asked if I needed food. I replied, "yes" and he said that supper would be served at 6:00 p.m. He showed me to the ladies dorm and assigned me to a bed and explained the procedures as well as introduced me to the rest of the residents. My first night was comfortable; I took a bath and bedded down. Early the next morning I was awakened by the turning on of lights and a woman walking through rousing other residents that had come in after I had fallen asleep. I think I went to sleep at about 7:00 p.m., because I did not want to be drowsy when it was time to get up and go out.

Well, it was the 4th of January and I enrolled myself in an H.E.A.R.T/N.T.A. program and in late January was called in to attend an interview. I went and was informed that I was expected to pay a fee, find my own uniform which was sold by the association, buy books and school supplies, as well as pay for transportation. I panicked, but spoke to my mentor from the Gleaner Company—he helped me with an extra $200 which I put with my vending profits, and purchased a blouse and skirt. He also told me to talk to someone at the Parish Council. Well I went back to the director who informed me that he could help. I had been attending classes five days per week and vending on Saturdays and Sundays to pay for transportation.

All was well, as my social worker started funding my lunch and transportation and gave me a monthly allowance of $400 per month. This helped immensely as I had to buy, beg and coerce the public health clinic to help out with dressings for my ulcer on my residual (stump).

In sum, the overwhelming pattern in the above life stories reveals that deportees tended to be from the 1.5 generation of immigrants. Their parents came from the lower rungs of Jamaican society and while abroad their families became unstable, leaving children to suffer the negative consequences of living in inner city impoverished neighborhoods. First generation deportees were few but nevertheless products of the same downward mobility.

Although deportees tended to be males of Afro-Caribbean hue, yet at least one deportee was mulatto and two were females. Not all were sane, in some cases the experiences abroad made immigrants into mentally impaired persons, and yet one deportee attributed his deportation to experiences which began in Jamaica and were exacerbated later by experiences in the U.S.

Transnationalism and Deportees

The term "transnational" defined in the literature as "a person's self conscious awareness of belonging to communities which span the national boundaries of host and home societies" (Levitt 2000), did not describe the deportees interviewed. They were Jamaicans, but did not feel attached to any country—in the U.S. and England they encountered the full brunt of being impoverished and classified as inferior and in Jamaica their very own countrymen mimicked the moral panic which incurred deportation through the Patriot Act in America and similar acts in England. Additionally, before some deportees were able to develop transnational activities they were confined to psychiatric institutions or arrested.

Hence, the Jamaican public outcry that deportees were transmigrants who transferred hi-tech criminal ideas from abroad to Jamaica appeared to be imaginary. But nevertheless, the stigma was real to interviewed deportees who were prohibited by law from returning to the country from which they were deported.

Within local communities, deportees were not given any opportunity to implement foreign ideas as countrymen thought deportees' ideas were always criminal. Everything that happened to deportees in Jamaica revolved around their stigmatized transnational criminal identity that was first constructed in the various U.S. and English governmental policies which permitted deportation, and then supported in the unwelcoming claims countrymen made about deportees. In the absence of freedoms to return to the U.S., or England interviewed deportees were trapped in local communities and in many cases confined to nostalgic memories about living abroad. Infrequently their memories were agitated by small sums of foreign money mothers sent, and in a couple of cases when a girlfriend or wife came from the U.S. to visit. Below, the life stories of Mark and Chris are used to illustrate these stigmatizing experiences of deportees:

Mark's Story
        In Jamaica I was processed through customs and then taken to the Central Police Station lock-up. I remained in lock-up for 4 hours because I did not have anyone to identify me. I gave them my father's address and told them that my father owned a house where I would be staying, so they released me. I remember when I went to take the bus to my father's house everything looked strange to me—the bus was crammed with people who were all looking at me as if I was going to take something from them. Some were whispering that I was a dirty deportee. I did not stay on the bus all the way to Mandeville, but came off at Williamsfield and walked to Bellfield.
        It was about 9:00 p.m. when I got home. My father had an old man keeping the house for him. When I opened the door there was no furniture in the house and the odor said that the old man was not taking care of his hygiene. I asked him where the bed was and he said that the furniture was stolen while we were in America.
        I recall sleeping on the floor. I left prison with US$40 which they converted to Jamaican dollars at the Central Police Station. After paying my bus fare, I had a few hundred dollars left. I gave the old man some of it. The next morning I went to see some friends that I had before I migrated, but they had also migrated. My grandparents had died while I was in prison. I went to see one of my cousins—she was glad to see me, but things changed when she asked me for money and I could not give it to her. She complained that I was mean and cheap. The little money I had did not last me much time and so I returned to my father's house to find the old man cooking dumplings and green bananas. I ate the bananas, but not the dumplings, because I did not trust his hygiene. Anyway, the old man left to take care of some business.
        I was now living alone, broke and with no one to turn to. In these days phones were not common and I wanted to call Mom or Dad in America to ask them to send me some money, but did not have the money to call them. There were a few banana trees in the yard and so I would eat boiled bananas and banana porridge. It was rough going. I stayed indoors. I was hiding because I knew what people were going to say. Mom sent me a box at Christmas with rice, peas, some canned fish and US$100. I went to Mandeville and bought a pair of shoes and a few other things. I saw one of my school friends who said he heard that I was back and would get me a job. I agreed. The first day on the job was disastrous, because all the folks there were wondering who this foreigner was who came to wash yams and was not in the office as a top man. I

was so embarrassed that I did not go back because I always wanted to stay out of trouble. December ended and it was now January. I had to return to eating bananas and drinking water and thank God that I was free and alive. I started to do a little farming. I planted some sweet potatoes which should take three months to mature. But at two months I was digging them up for food.

My sight was dark—because of the farming and the poor food I could hardly see. One day in May 1993, while farming, I felt a sharp pain in the right side of my belly. I had to drop my hoe and call out. I awoke to find myself in hospital with needles in my veins and a tube in my nose. After the pain was gone they took me to the University [teaching] hospital in Kingston where they ran tests and said they had to operate on me.

That night I jumped out of the window and fled. I walked all the way from Kingston to Mandeville in the hospital gown because I was so afraid they were going to cut me—I knew that I only had gas from starving. Dad had a friend with a grocery store who told me to not be afraid to ask for anything I wanted. I didn't take any cooking stuff from him, but still my bill was so big that the man stopped crediting me goods. It took me two years to pay off the bill. Anyway, in 1996 I went to pursue a DJ career in Spanish Town. I had learned to DJ and sing while in prison. I spent one year at studio there called Jump Fence, but each time I went for an audition they told me to come back next month.

I saw Luciano [a famous Reggae artiste] and he told me to go to Kingston. I did so, but did not find him, instead I found a studio in Papine, Kingston, called Kingston Music. I recorded 5 songs for the boss. He liked my music, but the rest of the people of the studio were jealous because I was a top DJ and they were slow and the boss was going to bus me. They told him that I was a deportee and I will let my friends come and rob and kill him. The boss called me to his office and said he did not know that I was a deportee and did not desire such people around him. He told me he was going to scratch my music. He used to pay me J$3,000 a week to stay in studio, but he did not give me a cent when he fired me.

I did not return to the country because I did not want to go back as a loser. I started to hang around other studios, but did not succeed. In 1999 I entered the Red Label Wine Song Competition and my face was on TV, in the *Star* [major Jamaican tabloid] and *Jamaica Gleaner* [the main Jamaican daily newspaper]. I did not get first place in the competition, but second place. People started to accept me and I was getting a few shows, but I did not understand the music business very well so I just wrote some songs and DJ'ed to myself. I also got a job with a fellow on a circus, but the moment I talked like a American he fired me.

In 2001 I started a little shop which lasted less than a month, because I had to get out of it—the people in the town said they could not take the noise and that my parents would be against it. So I had to pull down this dance hall after one year. In 2003 I wrote two job applications to Windalco in Kirkvine, but I never got a response. People in the plant probably told the administration that I was a bad influence. My father used to work in the plant, and they said if your father used to work there, the son can't get a job—tough luck for me. At present I'm at home. I get a few days work once in a while. I am really tired of looking for a job and I hate to be turned down. People in Jamaica don't like deportees and every minute my neighbor plays the deportee song by famous Reggae artist Buju Banton:

In the case of Chris when his girlfriend paid a visit to Jamaica, they rekindled their physical relationship in a cousin's house. However, months later on, his acts of cohabitation were retold to the owner of the house who had returned from farm work in Canada; this owner objected vociferously and required that Chris buy him a new bed. This existing one was defiled by Chris who performed restricted primal acts of cohabitation with a strange woman. The owner graphically described and demonstrated these offending acts to substantiate how much his cousin had declined by adopting American culture and also transporting these practices back to Jamaica.

To other relatives, Chris had spent upwards of twenty years abroad but had not made use of his opportunity. Instead he had wasted his time and resources on a following of "big bottom American girls," who wanted nothing more than his money. To his relatives it was not of importance that Chris had sold drugs, but that he did not have the transnational sense to send some of his money to Jamaica to be saved. From Chris's standpoint, his drug sales were not substantial. But, his relatives felt differently—coming from poverty Chris should have maintained a Jamaican identity of being miserly instead of feeding his acquired American life style.

The stigmatized criminal identity of deportees made it difficult for them to form friendships. Consequently, deportees tended to value their few friendships which did not last for very long. James recalled how on his first job as a tree cutter in Jamaica, all of laborers who started working together would talk during break time, but over time cliques formed. He left this tree cutting job and went to work on odd jobs as he did not want to face the sad feelings from lost relationships which reminded him of living in America.

At times the few ties which deported migrants developed did not meet the expectations of their parents who lived abroad. For example, Mark lived with his common law wife in Jamaica, but his father who lived in the U.S. said that she was not the best for him, and Mark should find someone who will be able to cook for him [Mark's father] when he returns to Jamaica. In response Mark disregarded his father's wish, taking the hard nose position that it was this woman who helped him after being deported to Jamaica. The individuals, with whom Mark's father wanted him to develop friendships, shunned him as a deportee. Not all deportees were sane and so their ability to participate in transnational relations was non-existent. However, among the insane some of their life changing experiences from abroad seeped into their lives. Take the case of James, he nearly stabbed a man who offered him a cigarette which smelt like the drugs which friends used to catalyze his first psychotic episode in New York:

> I did not have any plans to be in jail in Jamaica, but I am in jail now for stabbing a guy. I don't remember stabbing him though. I do not know the guy. I needed a draw off a cigarette and asked him for one, but he said this is the only one he had. The cigarette was laced with drugs and I knocked him out. I know the taste; it was just like my first taste of angel dust mixed with cocaine.

Countrymen's Perceptions of Deportees

To countrymen, the term deportee was a catch-all label for used Japanese motor cars and humans alike that were unwanted by foreign countries, but yet imported into Jamaica. Whether the term applied to criminal deportees or motor cars, it was disparaging. For example, Jamaican citizens identified deportee cars to be cheap in cost, inferior in quality and the drivers of these cars as aggressive, lower class cads to be excluded from middle class Jamaican society.

Human deportees were seen in a similar light for, at the very least, countrymen still expected them to have achieved economic mobility abroad. Since deportees had not met this expectation, they were perceived to be socioeconomic failures and criminals who were not deserving of re-entry into Jamaican social life and not worth mentioning in the same breath along with other groups of citizens. They were deemed by middle class Jamaicans to have a separate inferior culture which inhibited their re-entry into Jamaican life.

Countrymen, especially in rural communities, saw it as their right to monitor deportees and approve of their every activity. Some local inner-island country communities used their hyper-vigilance as a partial explanation for the absence of criminal deportees in their towns and the lack of same vigilance for the convergence of criminal deportees in the parishes of Portland, Kingston and St. Catherine.

Although not every deportee was a criminal, and though not every Jamaican had been injured by a deportee, the prevalence of negative talk about deportees conjured up widespread fears about them being responsible for super elevated levels of organized criminality. Even if deportees lived quietly, they were suspected to be consultants who were using their overseas contacts to construct international cocaine markets, or instructing willing others in organized crime and credit card fraud.

One well known criminal deportee, Bubba Smith, was an example of a deportee whose story was used to stigmatize all deportees:

> Oliver "Bubba" Smith, was deported from the U.S. in 2002 after living 8 years in New York. In Jamaica he pursued his life of crime by using skills learned in New York to take over small gangs and build a syndicate called the "One Order" gang, which until he was killed in July, dominated Spanish Town's crime world. The gang is aligned with the Jamaica Labor Party and is in constant battle with the People's National Party affiliated "Clansman" gang. Smith was also wanted by the police for masterminding the JA$3 million robbery of a Super Plus Food Store. (*Jamaica Gleaner*, February 9, 2006).

To justify their stigmatization of deportees where there was no clear evidence for doing so, countrymen constructed their version of stories. For example, Neville was supposed to be a psychiatric case, a man who came home one night and caught his wife with another man and killed her. However, from Neville's story, it was not his wife but his mate's girlfriend who was accidentally killed in a car he was driving.

Deportees were seen as anomalies to be explained. In Jamaica generations of people tended to maintain one place of residence for extended periods of time which gave deportees very little opportunity to be anonymous in rural communities. Where deportees moved among relatives, they were chastised for having failed abroad. If deportees resettled in a community where they were unknown, news eventually spread from their old community about their deportation.

From my interview with Neville, I gleaned evidence of the extent to which deportees were poorly received, excluded, and monitored by countrymen. He constantly remarked that, even though our conversation was not of anybody's business, yet people made it theirs, and in the morning the shop keeper would be enquiring from him about me. All deportee activities were deemed clandestine, and communities kept themselves safe by monitoring strangers and those who deportees talked with. At the end of our conversation, countrymen shouted treats at Neville. The communities left no anomalies about deportees unexplained.

Deportees had a very difficult time regaining entry into Jamaican communities because they were identified as potential criminals by countrymen who already knew about their predicament of being deported or deciphered it from their sudden reappearance from abroad with no accumulated capital, car or house.

On occasion, the unconscious use of a foreign accent by deportees was used by potential employers to adjudicate laborer job positions. Deportees reported that as laborers they were not paid equally with other countrymen. Take the case of James who recounted that his own uncle refused to pay him an agreed sum because his uncle felt deportees should be paid less than the going rate of pay. James recounted that when employers refused to pay, he silently walked away. In another case Neville reported that whenever homeowners wanted their difficult electrical jobs completed they came to him, but they were always unwilling to pay him as they would other laborers. For Neville he always ended up trading his valued professional knowledge for food items and payment of past debt.

When assistance was offered to homeless deportees at an organizational level, it was done through poor relief institutions which offered mental health evaluation, food, simple job duties and night shelter. An example was the Montego Bay Homeless and Street People Program.

Deportation taught deportees the realities of living abroad and coming home without any capital. For the first time they realized that social structures were unforgiving and made no distinction between hardened criminals and drug offenders. This treatment angered deportees because they thought the U.S. government should have been given them a second chance. When asked if they would return to America the sentiment was, "no." Not because America did not offer more material resources, but that the system did not give them any chances as non-violent, first-time offenders. Interviewed deportees felt as if they would have been better off not leaving Jamaica at all.

The Effects of Deportees' Mobility

Deportees tended to not accumulate much transferable material wealth abroad and on returning to Jamaica occupied the lower socio-economic reaches of Jamaican society. Survival in Jamaica meant occupying family homes, and receiving small amounts of money from their mothers who were still abroad.

At times there were relatives already living in these homes and deportees were permitted to live there, but in two cases relatives rejected the deportees. In

Cecile's case, rejection came from her mother who had been cruel to her abroad. And there was the case of Rudolph who went back to his family home but cousins who were living there ran him off. Rudolph's account was different from the police report which stated that he chopped his cousin with a machete. But, in Rudolph's story it was after he cut down a banana tree that his cousin called the police. For those deportees who did not have access to their family's old homes in rural communities, they migrated to urban areas such as the city of Montego Bay where life on the streets was particularly miserable, as they had to: sleep in homeless shelters, become dependent on welfare, and protect themselves physically from the abuse of countrymen who felt as though the deportees were the worst persons, since they were homeless after having been to the promised land abroad, but returned with nothing.

The significance of deportation is exemplified by Joseph, a deportee who owned his home, but lived on the streets where he was beaten by countrymen. Currently, although he lives in his house, he still eats lunch at the parish food pantry. Joseph met his American wife in Jamaica, married her and moved to America. Eventually their marijuana use led to cocaine use—Joseph's wife went to drug treatment but Joseph did not as he found the suggestion absurd. They separated and Joseph went to live with an African American Woman, but was arrested and deported to Jamaica penniless and living on the streets. He tried drug treatment, but failed a couple of times. Being "clean", now he volunteers his time to a boy's club, teaching them to play woodwind and brass instruments. Despite his experiences, Joseph reported that both of his past lovers have come to Jamaica to visit him and he expected his wife to bring their children for a visit in coming months.

The two female deportees appeared to be at extremes of the homeless return migration spectrum in that one was completely dependent on the homeless shelter for food and prescribed medications and the other was very industrious—attending school, while selling newspapers and mirrors.

In the absence of material resources to complete rites of return passage which are necessary for negotiating re-entry into Jamaican life, the skills, and material resources that deportees' parents acquired before leaving Jamaica came in handy. For example, Mark who lived in his parent's family home enclosed a portion of the large front yard and rented it out for dances. But, having some place to live rent free did not meet the community's standards for re-acceptance into community life. In the case of Samuel, he chose to meet expectations by constructing his own house, even though he lived in his grandmother's house. The acquisition of a professional skill was also vital to negotiation of re-entry. In the case of Neville who was not a certified electrician but knew aspects of the profession, he was able to borrow money from members of the community and when they needed work he would do it. Another example was Olivive who knew how to use the computer, and so the welfare program in Montego Bay bought one for her to do some administrative tasks at the homeless shelter. During the days rather than loaf, Olivive also sold mirrors. The chief complaint deportees made about the governments of America and Jamaica was they should have invested in the skill-training of deportees.

Those deportees, who came from families that owned businesses, were spoken about like voluntary returned residents, since they had resources to satisfy local community expectations of building of large homes, driving flashy new cars, and give away money. If their resources do not last, then this foothold still gave way to a poor reception. This was true of Bobby who splurged after arriving home, but resorted to crediting goods for which he did not pay—that was the point at which return migration really fell apart. But, Bobby felt that the community was jealous of his farm and devised every means to show him in poor light. For this reason Bobby reported that he only spoke with older male return migrants from England who were suffering the same experiences and to people outside of his community. Bobby related one notable incident, in which the police had to intervene. He hired a man to dig 200 yam holes, but this employee wanted to receive payment without having completed the contracted job.

To countrymen, Bobby was not being truthful about his deportee status, and wanted to live as if he was a voluntary return migrant.

DISCUSSION

Deportee return migration experiences were complex and varied. Nevertheless, all left Jamaica with low-colonial capital. Abroad they experienced downward socio-economic shifts from: poor individual choices; being mentally impaired; living with single female headed households in inner cities where immigrants of African ancestry become excluded from full participation in U.S. and English societies, initially for racial reasons, and then for criminal reasons.

Upon returning to Jamaica deportees who lacked wealth, were excluded from community life, access to jobs, and the rungs of middle class Jamaican society. Countrymen expect return migrants to bring home enough wealth to liberate themselves from public sector employment, create businesses and most of all provide evidence of success by building large multi-storied houses. Meeting these expectations did not confer any permanent status, as return migrants had to be always ready to meet the demands of other Jamaicans who needed money on the spur of the moment.

As a consequence of these rites of passage that deportees could not participate in, they were denied the opportunity to negotiate re-entry into Jamaican society. Instead, deportees lived on the edge of social activities and relationships. The boundaries of deportee activities were maintained through high levels of scrutiny which local communities applied. This close scrutiny robbed deportees of the freedom to implement transnational ideas, or invent stories which heightened their social esteem among peers.

Given the above discussion, this research does not support a conclusion which argues that deportees were transnationals. Instead it appears that the effect of transnationalism on deportee return migration was over exaggerated by countrymen and in anecdotal newspaper reports.

This research lends support to the findings of Griffin 2000; Austin 2003; and Headley 2005 which argue that not all deportees were transnational masterminds. The deportee criminal identity was first constructed in the U.S. and English deportation policies and then became part of Jamaicans' mass hysteria about deportees. Deportees' migration fell apart primarily because of their extremely low colonial capital and associated factors such as poor parental supervision, their mental capacity, involvement in drug peddling activities which deterred their mobility, and some were just too young to construct their own success abroad.

One could construct a theoretical statement arguing that deportee return migration was affected by their colonial capital at the time of migration. More specifically by their low: financial capital; social graces; family relations and stigmatized criminal identity.

CHAPTER FOUR
Colonial Capital Matters:
A Comparison of Voluntary & Involuntary Return Migrants

This chapter revisits the life stories previously used, and focuses on the activities migrants performed. I first look at mid- and high-colonial capital voluntary return migrants, and make comparison with deportees. The patterns that are generated will then be used to improve the theoretical understandings about return migrants and especially deportees; a group slighted in return migration literature.

Understanding migrants' lives before they migrated is pivotal, as the activities they performed then, helped to determine their outcomes abroad and on returning to Jamaica. In all cases interviewees had some support from relatives when they migrated and when they returned to Jamaica, but in contrast to high-colonial capital migrants, the stories of migrants with low- and mid-colonial capital reveal that they had little or no financial help from their parents. As a consequence, during childhood migrants with mid-colonial capital had to work to sustain their families, and this stymied improvements in their education and social graces. Victor's story, a migrant whose family had low-colonial capital illustrates this:

> We knew what it meant to be poor. My father who was a tailor always rented a shop in a neighboring town to carry out his trade. Every fortnight one of my tasks was to walk bare footed for 12 miles, to and fro, on unpaved rock-stone roads to collect the family allowance of maybe five shillings.
>
> My mother kept a little 'higgler shop' and my second major task was to help her to run the shop as she had failing eyesight for many years. So from the age of about eight years, each Thursday, she sent me on the market train in the company of the higglers to sell agricultural goods in Coronation Market. On Saturday mornings I bought goods for the shop and returned on the market train

by Saturday afternoon. I got home just in time to grab a bite and man a stall on the China Man shop piazza at Sandy Gutt. A high point of all this was that at age eight I knew all the wholesalers in Kingston and which items to buy from whom at the lowest price.

My third task was to take chocolate (dried cocoa beans) to sell at Cocoa Walk and return with a zinc pan of wet sugar to sell in mom's higgler shop. Carrying this zinc pan of sugar was sheer hell; it weighed about as much as a bag of cement and pushed my neck down in my shoulder. Consequently, at age fifteen I was only about forty inches tall.

I moved to Kingston at the age of fifteen to live with my elder sister who was settled there. I was apprenticed to R.E. Taylor of 117 Princess Street to learn French polishing at the princely wage of two shillings and six pence per week.

I was transferred to the furniture showroom with an increase in pay to five shillings per week. But, I had to earn more to meet all the family's needs. As a result I made handles for straw bags which I sold to the craft vendors in the Coronation Market. This was the mother of innovations as the only tools I had were a compass saw and a gimlet: I finished the handles with shoe polish as I had no facilities to do conventional finishing.

We moved house four times in the next year or so; the last was memorable. We could not afford to hire a hand-cart so we packed all our earthly possessions on our single bedspring and placed it on our heads, I in front and my sister in the rear. We set out in the beautiful moonlit night across the wastelands along the footpaths linking the neighboring communities

We made another move as we could now afford better accommodations. I left R.E. Taylor and was working with Mr. George DaCosta, because things were slow and I was not earning much. My sister was now working and had a helper taking care of her two children while she was at work. I contributed to the household expenses, but at times when there was no work I had no money, but my sister did not believe me, so she told her helper not to give me anything to eat. I went two full weeks without eating: after the first week I was so weak that I could not get out of bed; I told the other tenants in the yard that I was not feeling well. I could not tell them the truth as my sister, at this time, was better off than all of them.

Some good came out of this experience as when the facts were known the son of one of the tenants took me to his workplace—Jamaica Fruit and Shipping Company, where I was employed as a mail clerk at twenty five shillings per week.

This enabled me to get my own room and enjoy a little easier life. I was able to send regular gift packages by the country bus to my mother and enroll at Waltham College to do my Senior Cambridge. Mr. DaCosta offered me a challenging contract to make 150 Mahogany, Mahoe and Satin Wood stock width picture frames measuring only half an inch wide, for Tower Isle Hotel. At the end of this contract I was asked to make a full set of household furniture for a friend who was getting married. This was the stepping stone for me to start my own business in furniture manufacturing, furniture retailing, haberdashery and shoemaking.

The difference between Victor and other migrants with low-colonial capital is he found time to complete Senior Cambridge Exams, and this I would argue gave him mid-colonial capital status. Later on while living in England Victor found that furthering his education was a vehicle to gaining a profession and getting out of England quickly. In other cases mid-colonial capital migrants tried to improve themselves, and pave the way for their children through marriage. Reg realized quite early in life that skin pigmentation contributed to success and married a light skinned Jamaican woman, so as to increase his colonial capital, and that of his children. However, this route did not liberate him from spending 30 to 40 years abroad.

In contrast, migrants with high-colonial capital focused on attending school, while their parents performed the major income producing economic activities. Evidence is provided from Cleveland's story, as he did not want for anything because his parents provided all of his material needs:

> I was born in Kingston, Jamaica, and went to Mico Practicing Primary School at age 6, where my uncle was the headmaster. At age 11, I went to Excelsior High School, graduated at 17. I was a very happy person with no extremes in my life of riches or poverty, and I never pined after anything.

In the case of Hugh he went to school, and became a teacher. The work that he did for his father did not distract from school. Evidence is provided in the below excerpt:

> I went to the Charleton Infant School and Primary schools 2 miles away from home. I remember vivid school experiences at Charleton:
> In Grade 3, the principal said to the teacher, "that boy will never learn to write so leave him alone."
> In Grade 4 Mrs. Scott taught long division and this was difficult, so we charged other students one penny so that they would have the right answers also.
> In Grade 5, I learned woodwork and leather craft from Mr. Anderson. In Grade 6 I joined 4H Club and went over to the nearby reformatory school to learn how to cook pot roast. The skills learned in Grades 5 and 6 have been vital to my success in life. I did not pass Common Entrance in Grade 6 and so went on to grade 9.
> In Grade 7 the teacher I had was Mrs. Lawrence. I thought that I could sing and so joined the school choir. But, I was booted because I constantly spoiled the chorus. Life had its challenges because we had school inspection teams from the Ministry of Education and were expected to recite most school work verbatim. My early inclination for agriculture started on one of the excursions students took to Reynolds Jamaica Mines. It was in this Grade 7 I started to wear shoes to school and joined the Boys Brigade.
> In Grade 8 we received additional duties at home and started working on my father's shop and on his truck as every child got additional duties before going to school.
> In 1970, after completing Grade 9 I graduated. No, as a matter of fact, students did not have graduation ceremonies; we just left school in Grade 9. There was no Grade Nine Achievement Test then, only Technical Examination for technical college. At age 15 I was saved by my bigger sister who took me to Kingston to attend a private high school. Though I was in Kingston ever holiday I came home to help my father work on his truck. I did so well at this new school in 3rd form that my teachers put me into 4th form; in the same year.

The Ambivalence to Leave Jamaica

Although Jamaicans encouraged migration, interviewees with mid-colonial capital tended to migrate only after exhausting all possibilities and after devastating events, such as losing jobs, or all of their agricultural crops to natural disasters, like the 1952 Jamaican hurricane.

> *Reg's Story*
>
> People always encouraged me to go to England, but I always said no. In Jamaica, the only way to make money as a black boy was to farm or take up a trade. I noticed that one could not make enough money from farming, and after the 1952 hurricane the only people making money were those with a trade. I picked up cabinet making at my cousin's shop. But that did not make enough money so one day coming home from the field I made my decision to migrate.

In the case of Merissa, leaving Jamaica was justified as women felt fortunate to find a mate who had migrated to the Mother Country. In the below case of Victor, his factory was not netting enough money to support a growing family:

> On June 8th, 1950, I married Daisy, my wife, and by February 1954 we were blessed with three healthy boys. At this point business wasn't going as well as expected. I moved the factory three times, had difficulty getting electrical power for the three pieces of power tools I possessed, and money was not always readily available to meet the needs of my now growing family, so I decided to emigrate to England for 9 years; primarily to acquire more and better power tools.

In contrast, migrants with high-colonial capital were more cavalier about leaving.

> To initiate migration I just told my father, booked my passage and left for London in 1959. I did not have any assets except for a car which I sold.

Preservation of Resources

Mid-colonial capital voluntary return migrants were careful about not losing their accumulated wealth in Jamaica. Migration was a calculated effort to accumulate additional valued resources over a short period of work and then return to Jamaica. Mass migrants to England planned to achieve wealth and return to Jamaica within 5 years. Interviewed mid-colonial capital post-1965 migrants to America stayed long enough to earn needed cash over short 3 month work periods as nurses, or 3 to 15 year stays as students and laborers.

In preparation for returning in the future, migrants who owned land and businesses in Jamaica did not sell, but left them under the control of relatives. Others who did not own land dreamed of earning enough money to purchase property in Jamaica.

Migrants imagined a positive change in their mobility abroad, and celebration of their new wealth and imparting of a better way of life to countrymen. An example of this sentiment was Angella who stated, "We went abroad to show whites that blacks could be successful too. And we came back to teach other Jamaicans to be better."

The Experience of Shock

On actually arriving abroad, all interviewed voluntary return migrants were shocked at the cold weather, and job conditions in foreign countries. Migrants who had mid-colonial capital were extremely shocked that simply being in a foreign country, in and of itself, did not catapult them out of poverty, as they were routinely denied access to wealth, good housing, and excluded from opportunities located in the dominant parts of host societies. Their status was not determined by current activities performed, but presumed to be inferior because of their African ancestry and being from a slave colony. Even migrants with high-colonial capital were disappointed. Take the case of Cleveland, he was disappointed in the labor jobs that were provided since he came from Jamaica with managerial work experience. And Hugh in the extract below could not find a teaching job:

> I needed cash quickly and migrated to the U.S. in 1986. I thought that since I was a teacher in Jamaica, I could probably find a teaching job there. But then the reality set in when I couldn't get a good job. They wanted to hire me as a para-professional and this was a rude awakening. I then took a job as a horticultural plant technician to water office plants. They paid me US$6 and this was more than what the government was willing to pay.

In many ways migrants experienced the very same identity and poverty issues they thought were left in Jamaica. Some mid-colonial capital migrants beat a hasty retreat, or like Reg sent their children back to school in Jamaica after they realized the realities of foreign cultures. But, soon these same migrants either returned abroad or constructed transnational alliances with those who remained abroad, because they had not accrued enough resources to exit their previous role and identity as poor in Jamaica.

Successful migration and return migration, they found, had to be planned and executed over an indefinite number of years and by adopting miserliness. In so doing, mid-colonial capital migrants who went to England seldom visited Jamaica (maybe 4 times in 30 to 40 years), and made hard choices to remain abroad even when loved ones died. Angela recalled that when her father died in Jamaica she did not have enough money to attend the funeral or to bury him. She had to borrow money from neighbors whom she repaid over time.

To achieve enough initial capital, migrants with mid-colonial capital worked in multiple low wage jobs, lived together in one room tenements, and denied themselves consumer purchases. Migrants in England also transferred survival strategies such as "Pardner" from Jamaican culture. In Pardner Jamaicans pooled their resources among themselves by depositing sums of money over extended periods of time. At pre-determined intervals each person in the group would take turns receiving the total pool of money—called a hand. British Banks did not understand this system for banks paid interest on savings but Pardners did not. However, the advantage was that when the hand was drawn there was no need for a loan from British financial institutions, which did not support Jamaican migrants anyway (Phillips et al. 1998). By and large, these mid-colonial capital migrants did not have the necessary trust for British financial institutions and so saved money under their mattresses and sent remittances to Jamaica to be saved by relatives. The disposition to work in low wage jobs, transfer legal ideas from Jamaica, maintain family commitments, save, and pay bills were seminal to their success. As will be seen, these qualities differentiated voluntary return migrants with mid-colonial capital from migrants who became deportees.

Migrants in the sample with high-colonial capital did not face the need to own houses, as they planned to return home quickly, and so lived rent free with parents or siblings. In Cleveland's case he lived in his parents' home for three years, and Hugh lived with his brother rent free for a year in New York.

The paths that voluntary returnees with different colonial capital cut from the racist social fabric had to do with the social graces each used to confront racism. Returnees with mid-colonial capital reported fighting English coworkers who offended them. In one migrants story he cut off the tie of a bartender who refused to serve him. In another case, a returnee punched his coworker who allowed sewage from a plumbing line to soil his person. But, migrants with high-colonial capital did not use physical force and were more tactful as in the below extract from Cleveland's story:

> On my third job, the English employees went out together, and I felt excluded. I went to my boss, expressed my desire to leave because of being excluded. To my surprise, my boss said I should not leave. Today I still correspond with some of my co-workers from this job over these many forty years through Christmas cards. Even when I left, England a coworker and his wife came to the wharf to say goodbye.

Remaining for extended periods meant migrants experienced assimilation. Reg experienced assimilation on his second job when he started to understand English slang, and Winnie, when he went to College in the U.S. and became a member of the football team. Some who remained abroad for 30 to 40 years and were married resisted assimilation aggressively by divorcing their spouses, who they thought were acting in ways which would not make return possible. In so doing these migrants reaffirmed their unfeigned commitment to returning home. However, tackling the effects of foreign cultures was an ongoing process as couples had to confront this issue on returning to Jamaica, for females continued to look very favorably at their lives abroad.

Repatriation 30 to 40 years or 7 to 15 Years Later

Taking the first step to return was sometimes calculated and sometimes catalyzed by unexpected events. More often than not voluntary return migrants with higher education and some wealth were the ones who returned within an expected time. This was true of Victor who returned from England in 15 years, Hugh who returned from the U.S. in 9 years and Cleveland who returned from England in 7 years.

Mid-colonial capital migrants who only achieved economic success came home 30 to 40 years later after reaching retirement or after unexpected events. One unexpected event which forced migrants to make decisions was early retirement. Some returnees were surprised that they could retire early at the suggestion of their employer. This was true of John who worked as a postal clerk and benefited from changes in employment policies. The postal agency offered early retirement packages to employees who had health benefits and employed contract workers who would not be provided with these costly benefits.

In other cases returnees had the misfortune of retiring because of ill-health. Take the case of Merissa's husband who migrated to England in search of greater income and a more equitable society. While in England he first worked as a painter. Finally in his twilight years, he managed to get a government job as a hospital porter, but after ten years was diagnosed with lung cancer. On the advice of his doctor he came home to enjoy breathing clean air. This illness cost him, as he had to wait ten years before receiving his pension.

Whatever their reasons were for deciding to leave, mid-colonial capital returnees who spent 30 to 40 years funded their return and were ambivalent about returning home. But they were also gleeful about completing their migration cycle by returning to the warm climate of home, where among other things they could enjoy their pensions and "sweet, sweet Jamaica."

Besides figuring out what to take home and how to afford return, migrants remained perplexed about which image of Jamaica to believe: the negative images portrayed in the media of Jamaicans being criminals who sabotaged their own success, conflicted with their nostalgic memories of Jamaica. The conflict over what to believe about Jamaica remained unresolved, even after returning to Jamaica.

Once the decision to return was reached, mid-colonial capital returnees who remained abroad for 30 to 40 years, tended to receive news through formal institutions. English returnees had a well developed number of associations in England and Jamaica which disseminated information about the pitfalls in returning. Migrants also received information from the British Consulate about life in Jamaica and receipt of their pension benefits. Returnees from England felt as if they were still truly Jamaicans, and imagined how to demonstrate to countrymen that they had finally exited the role of poor Jamaican. This disposition left many returnees vulnerable to being fleeced by investment institutions, lawyers, family and friends.

Return migrants with high-colonial capital were not ambivalent. Those who pursued educational goals consulted the Jamaican High Commission to find jobs and those like Hugh who really went abroad to get investment capital for existing businesses periodically sent home goods and money. What is of sociological significance is the financial investment and involvement of parents and relatives in the return lives of migrants with high-colonial capital, and the stability of their occupations in Jamaica. In the case of Cleveland, previous to returning to Jamaica his father bought him a car and in recent years willed him several rental houses in Jamaica. Cleveland also held the same job in Jamaica from 1966 and recently retired from a chief position. Hugh returned to the gas station his father had helped him to purchase, and as I interviewed him the buzz of conversations indicated that his aunts and relatives abroad were involved financially. Besides the gas station, Hugh was a Justice of the Peace, Chairman for the local all-age school board and was involved in computer skills training to produce more capable workers.

Other returnees in the sample with high-colonial capital maintained close contact with Jamaica to ensure they would not consider themselves as ever having been away, and were involved in local community life: Goodwin stated, "I do not give them a chance to think that I was ever away by dressing differently or talking differently." Dorothy went to the U.S. to earn a Masters in Psychology and returned because she was in Jamaica so often that it made sense to stay. She owned minibuses and computer training centers. Janice was a nurse who worked as she felt necessary to accomplish financial stability in Jamaica. Her longest nursing job in America was for six months.

This is where the return paths of migrants with high-colonial capital stopped as they remelded into Jamaican society as countrymen. However, the paths of returnees who had remained abroad for 30 to 40 years continued into shock and transnationalism.

The Nexus Between Mid-colonial Capital and Transnationalism

On actually returning to Jamaica, mid-colonial capital returnees who remained abroad for 30 to 40 years soon found that their transnational bifocal identity as both foreigner and Jamaican became a source of their sadness and exclusion from countrymen. Frequently returnees prefixed their statements with, "When I was abroad…" and this irked countrymen who often responded, "then why don't you go back," and "nobody can come change Jamaica."

Returning home was a journey of despair for returnees' personal identities were subsumed by their social identity as "English" or "Yankee." Returnees recognized their zero sum gain: in England they were excluded because they had low education, and were black, but on returning were excluded because they had adopted white English tea time, the discipline of time, odd ways of dressing, cockney accents, were black, had low education, and did inferior jobs. Returnees in this category from the U.S. were seen as arrogant. These shifts were not welcomed as Jamaican society had experienced national identity shifts from emulating British culture to being influenced strongly by black American pop culture. It was during this stage of returning that the shifts in returnees identity became poignant and returnees realized how much of their dreams of home were imagined, and predicated on transferring ideas from abroad to a society that had not remained static; as it was in their minds.

Goods that they thought would be needed to establish their wealthy successful returnee identity in Jamaica, such as new motor cars, and furniture were already available in abundance to the poor, and at lower rates than returnees could ever imagine.

Some mid-colonial capital returnees who spent 30 to 40 years abroad lost touch with the reorganization of Jamaican social life through their many years abroad said, "If we had visited before actually returning then we would not have come back," and "the only reason for not returning abroad is the feeling of shame." Harold blamed the British High Commission, and the Jamaican government for painting a pretty picture of Jamaica. On the surface this assignment of blame appeared absurd: didn't returnees acquire information from others about Jamaica before returning? Yes, they were privy to information about returning, but their commitment to Jamaica and the intensity to which they held on to their nostalgic dreams of Jamaica did not permit them to understand the gravity of returning and that returnees were only welcomed for their foreign currency.

By free will or force, Jamaicans extracted financial capital from returnees through high level financial institutional fraud, robbery, and exorbitant rates for goods and services. Several return migrants were subjected to brutal rapes and robberies immediately on arriving home from the airport. The criminal schemes were reported to start at the airport where the names and addresses of returning residents were copied from their luggage tags or passports and then relayed by cell phone to an ally. On arriving at their residence assailants greeted return residents in a friendly manner and by name before committing their crimes. For example, "Hi Paul, it has been a long time since I have seen you."

Mid-colonial capital returnees discovered the flaws in their plans much too late; they had gained economic success abroad, but lost intimate ties with their left-behind children forever. In one reported case, although a female returnee had children, she had to live with her niece in Kingston because her children claimed they did not know her as a mother. Though the returnee eventually moved from her niece's home to live near to her children in Montego Bay they did not even visit her. The niece of the returnee found it interesting that the returnees' children visited her in Kingston, some 100 miles away, but did not visit their mother who lived a stones throw away. Eventually this returnee heeded advice by moving to a connected community where fellow returnees lived.

It was as if disappointment was unavoidable, as even those mid-colonial capital migrants who had planned their return and maintained strong informational ties with relatives, felt that countrymen took every opportunity to fleece and reject returnees. In the words of Reg, the word returnees are spelt with three Ms: they were mean, had money, and were mad.

Making Return Viable, Amidst Fear of Crime and Discord

Faced with a plethora of difficulties, migrants who spent 30 to 40 years abroad saw the value in maintaining strong transnational ties. This was particularly useful to women as they tended to prefer their lives abroad where they experienced structural advantages.

Out of their feelings of vulnerability which came from frequent talk about crimes, and knowing that there was little police protection, fully pensioned retirees took further transnational counter measures to insure themselves by leaving some of their pension in foreign financial institutions. This also optimized their income in Jamaica each time the Jamaican currency devalued.

Talk of crime and transnational activities did not deter any returnee from building conspicuous, multi-storied homes which dwarfed neighboring countrymen's homes. Why, some Jamaicans asked? Returned residents from England explained that they were denied access to modern housing in England, the houses in England that they finally bought were very small and they grew up in small homes. Now that money was not a big issue, they were providing the space they had always wanted to accommodate visiting relatives and church brethren from abroad. By building luxury homes, returnees celebrated their personal liberation from their past experiences of living in rooms with six other persons, from needing to turn down their music, or asking whites for permission to buy or rent houses.

Large homes symbolized that returnees had won economically, and through the size of houses were celebrating their returnee identity and financial achievements. The house size also marked the end of their migration cycle. As one resident stated, "I got what I went to England for—a house—and now my house is bigger than my neighbor's." Goodwin from America said, "building this house was my dream, that is why I went abroad to fulfill this boyhood dream." Mid-colonial capital return migrants left with little or no financial capital and came back with wealth, some of which they accumulated by selling their homes abroad.

Despite their bravado, the talk of crime made returned residents distrustful of countrymen, hyper-vigilant about people and made some feel imprisoned in their own homes. Hyper-vigilance was exhibited in returned residents going home before nightfall, driving past their gates before actually driving in and checking to make sure that dogs were acting in usual ways before entering their luxury houses. In the week that I visited the returned residents in May Pen, their association building was robbed of its food provisions.

In addition to information from other returned residents, sample official reports shown below, from the British High Commission contributed to making returnees fearful:

> In view of the high levels of crime and violence including kidnapping, and in the light of recent incidents involving British nationals, you should follow these common sense guidelines: Be particularly alert for thieves. You are advised against walking at night or using public transport. Only taxis authorized by the Jamaica Union of Travelers Association and ordered from hotels for your sole use (i.e. unshared) should be used.

Source: British High Commission Internet Website.

The returned residents negotiated their fear of crime by not living in their community of origin; not making down payments on construction jobs or sending money for construction purposes to their relatives or lawyers and by not keeping any cash in their homes. Harold felt if one made a down payment on a job the contracted person would take the down payment without completing the job.

Some eased into rural community life by building a house years in advance of actually returning, and created friendship ties within this community. However, building luxurious homes in rural communities was not encouraged as this practice proved fatal for some. Instead potential returnees were encouraged by other returnees and various Jamaican Building Societies to purchase lots of land in connected subdivisions.

While living within subdivisions increased personal protection, yet it also increased the unlikely readjustment to the wider Jamaican communities. This was so as in subdivisions returned residents were surrounded by others who created activities to reinforce their ways of living abroad. For example, neighborhood watches made returnees feel safe, as if they were living abroad, but these neighborhood watches also aided the social exclusion of returned migrants from countrymen who felt labeled as potential criminal elements to be watched.

To gain distance from people in their communities of origin, when paying visits, some returnees who remained abroad for 30 to 40 years hired unrecognizable taxi cabs and left their car at home. On their infrequent visits returnees handed out small sums of money to their impoverished relatives, but did not go into their relatives homes.

Despite these security measures, returnees still became targets because of their ostentatious houses, dress and accents were a dead give away. To countrymen, mid-colonial capital returnees who remained abroad for many years had lost their ability to determine who was trustworthy. Hence, to my informant most of the reported crimes against returnees were considered trivial by others and deemed to have resulted from returnees own lack of good judgment. To the returnees, however, no crime was trivial and they felt targeted and unprotected by the police.

Not all returnees who remained abroad for 30 to 40 years avoided their community of origin. Some were so intent on wanting to make fellow Jamaicans better that they evoked responses such as, "go back where you come from." These offended returnees brought remedy to their exclusion in Jamaica by living in enclaves with housing associations, and forming associations which provided the same social support as in Britain through indulgent creative outlet with fellow returned migrants (Goulbourne 1999). Participation in associations eased their lives among countrymen who some returnees described as dull and monotonous. To emphasize her point, one interviewee asked me point blank, "have you ever tried to hold a conversation with a Jamaican? Day in, day out the conversation is about one thing, poverty, and not about ways to solve it."

Returnees also used their associations' dense transnational network to communicate with potential returnees about being prepared for life in Jamaica. This was of importance as many of the returnees who remained abroad for 30 to 40 years, with whom I spoke, did not have a computer, or email service to do their own communicating and research. They depended on the associations to make formal statements on their behalf (Goulbourne 1999).

Jamaica Is Nice When You Can Leave
Although mid-colonial capital interviewees were Jamaicans by birth, and citizenship, yet they passionately clung to their coveted British passports as it conferred immediate transnational access to countries which provided the conveniences of modern medical care, uncensored social activities and welcomed

temporary relief from life in Jamaica. To these returnees, maintenance of transnational ties was a rational decision. The thought of paying for hospitalization and medicine was unacceptable since mid-colonial capital returnees from England had grown accustomed to socialized medicine. In the case of Herby and Angela the thought of paying JA$12,000 each month for their medicine was unacceptable. To cope with these costs, fully pensioned returnees visited host countries frequently to stock up on supplies of free medicine and to treat ongoing illnesses. At this point in their lives they had medical conditions and made full use of their earned benefits abroad. For sick returned residents, life in Jamaica could be good if they had their good health. Going back to England for medical care, though, placed some returnees in roles which they though were left behind. Mid-colonial capital returnees who were dark skinned felt that in cases of major medical problems, they were placed on a medical waiting list, while lighter skinned returnees and English whites were attended to immediately.

In Jamaica, mid-colonial capital returnees' transnational identity and mobility afforded them the opportunity to live above the cusp of countrymen's rejection. These return migrants lived both socially and materially, all at the same time, in Jamaica, the U.S. and the U.K where they had investments (Basch et al. 1994:269). However, despite their economic freedoms, returned migrants who spent 30 to 40 years abroad were continuously affected by their low colonial capital. To some countrymen, returnees' continuous travel signaled that they had only built houses in Jamaica, but were really still living abroad. Returnees were perceived to be harboring mistrust of Jamaicans and their medical expertise. The rationale behind countrymen's reasoning was that the cost of airfare could buy comparable medical care in the Caribbean. But, returnees used their mobility to avoid being fleeced medically. Before actually accepting Jamaican doctors' diagnoses of medical conditions, they sometimes visited their doctors abroad. Returned migrants had learned that it was not beyond medical practitioners to create false illnesses or misdiagnose existing ones.

The Special Case of Deportees

In 1981, at age 16 after graduating high school in Jamaica, I went to join my mother in New York City because I wanted to be with her so badly. But, the relationship with my mother was poor, and she use to beat on me so much that I became a mental case. I ran away in the street, could not keep a job, lived in homeless shelters and ended up in hospitals because I had nowhere to go. I was very sad and wanted to commit suicide because I did not feel close to anybody. Everybody was cold, standoff and isolated. It was a lonely life and they told lies on me and I was deported.

The above excerpt from Cecile's story illustrates the distinct shifts and experiences involuntary returned migrants had abroad which set them apart from voluntary return migrants. Like Cecile, most deportees were 1.5 generation migrants who lived with inept mothers in inner city environs where their peers and poor decisions exposed them to drug use, homelessness, arrest, and eventual deportation.

Deportees shared pensioned return migrants' experience of being perturbed by abject poverty, doubt about their future economic success in Jamaica, and the hope for wealth and fully realizing their dreams abroad. On arriving abroad, like voluntary return migrants, deportees experienced being inferior blacks and realized that there was great discrepancy between their imagined world of expectations and the reality of poverty inner cities afforded them (Lofland and Stark 1965).

Shock: Recalculation of Migration

Clearly daily life and access to valued resources was not as it appeared when parents visited and sent barrels of goods home to them in Jamaica. In addition, migration became a big failure for deportees whose parents' separated and they were left vulnerable to peers. In the cases of Mark, James and Samuel their mothers required money from their children. It was at this turning point that deportee's pathway became differentiated from voluntary returnees, as the viable activities they pursued to remedy their economic disappointment, moved them from a conventional life style to one centered on novice deviancy (Heyl 1979). It was as if once deportees began to explore viable options in inner cities, they could not be saved from becoming deviants. Although parents chided deportees to avoid bad company they developed and maintained these contacts with peers who were already involved in deviant behavior. For example, James stated that, "my mother could not show me anything—when she tired talking I slammed the door in her face."

In so doing migrants who became deportees took the path of native born blacks (Portes et al. 1993) whose mobility was always in decline for structural reasons, or from their own decided exclusion from access to opportunities in the dominant culture (Waters 1999; Portes et al. 1993; Vickerman 1999). For deportees like Cecile who may have become mentally impaired in the U.S., her mother's reported beatings only encouraged her to run away from home.

Much of deportee delinquency began as risk taking (Short and Strobeck 1965), and in some cases, the spontaneous pursuit of fun provided the impetus for delinquency as participants did not always see their misconduct as criminal. Four interviewed deportees stated that the first time they took crack cocaine it was friends who laced their cigarettes—as a prank. After their prank use of crack cocaine deportees turned novice deviants who adopted a deviant subculture and identified fully with peers from whose perspective criminal behavior was acceptable (Heyl 1979).

The transition to novice deviant took deportees only short periods from the time of arrival to six months. In this sharp turn into a new life, deportees often dealt drugs which escalated into poorly planned criminal activity to escape the predicament of poverty and the future possibility of becoming like their parents who worked for paltry sums.

The social psychology of Adler's (1985:84) big-time dealers describes deportees' view of drug dealing as a viable counter to their downward shifts in mobility: When their lofty Jamaican dreams encountered the stark reality of economic decline in inner cities, they took to drug wheeling and dealing which provided an opportunity to live for the present with the maximum pleasures they could grab. They temporarily re-attained childlike expectations, as if they were in Jamaica, by escaping the unpleasant responsibilities of life abroad, while seizing the opportunity to surround themselves with anything money could buy. Take the case of Samuel, a deportee from the 1.5 generation of migrants:

> This was a turning point as the Rastas taught me things I needed to know, as a man, about the Great Pyramids, that blacks constructed them. A pure big things them deal with, they respected the philosophy of Marcus Garvey, loved money, sent all of their children to college, and drove Mercedes Benzes.
>
> This was a turning point, as I started to grow my hair. I always wanted to grow my hair, even when I lived in Jamaica I spent much time with a Rastafarian friend who had a sound system, and a restaurant. They were like my second home and I still call the man father. I have always been around Rastas and it was not strange to be working among them in the U.S.
>
> In 1993 to 1994, I attended middle school. It was not like Jamaica, even though lots of Jamaican attended, it was different. We did not wear uniforms which made it difficult to determine if we were going to school or work. School children drove their own vehicles and even stolen vehicles to school, smoked, drank liquor, and carried guns. And there were pronounced gangs from Haiti and Puerto Rico. There we had to unite to survive for by myself I was an outcast. Many days, on arriving at school I stood and wondered if I should enter the building or go walking because I did not know anybody. I felt out of place as in every class I had to tell my name. There wasn't anything enticing to make me want to go to school. I saw people who wanted to talk to me but conversations were casual. Most people were Jamaican, but I did not have a connection with them.
>
> My outsider feelings lasted for about 2 weeks, and Christmas 1993 was nice. I had a girlfriend and my brethren who lived in the basement of my apartment building owned a little sound system. We kept a basement party and invited friends from school for food and liquor. My mother and I paid for the food since she liked to cook food for friends. It was a joy for her to hear that I was keeping a party. This made me popular among Jamaicans.
>
> My mind strayed from school and after a while felt like I was missing and wanting. I felt like I wanted to go to the street to work and not ask my mother for money. I did not want to be caught up in one place every day. January 1994 I stopped going to school and started selling beef patties and marijuana in a little hole in the wall store owned by Boy.

The sharp turn that deportees made into deviance determined the brevity of their tenure abroad as free persons. Although deportees spent many years abroad, incarceration in correctional institutions, or mental institutions accounted for many of these years. In the sample of interviewees only two deportees amassed any wealth from their illegal activities and were free for any significant period. One such case was Samuel and the other was Bobby a first n deportee who lived and plied his trade for twenty years in England, and bought a house in Jamaica.

Their transition was aborted by arrest. However, there were anecdotal reports of deportees who became professional criminals even after returning home, but none lived in rural communities where interviews were completed.

Transition to a life of professional deviancy takes time to acquire the necessary skills for the efficient perpetration of deviant acts.

Forced Repatriation

Unlike voluntary returnees, deportees lost the right to plan their return migration. Their lives now revolved around managing their stigmatized identity and homelessness. Joseph recounted some of his experiences:

> In 1989 after my mother came back from America, she wanted to cry because I was on the street washing cars and eating out of the garbage cans. Life was rough. People said I robbed them and wanted to burst my head—often running me down to cut off my locks.

Deportees efforts to disconnect from who they had become in America and England were zero sum gains. Jamaican countrymen presumed deportee connections with gangs abroad and stigmatizing them as transnational criminals. The strong social networks in local communities denied deportees any opportunity to remain anonymous or even to perform identity work by fabricating self esteem enhancing stories; as done by homeless persons in Anderson et al. (1993). Deportees felt that returning from abroad without resources was worst than having remained in Jamaica and being poor.

It was clear from the collected life stories that deportee' activities and return path were constrained by their lack of improvement in any area of their lives, and the negative judgment that countrymen held about their colonial capital. As a consequence, countrymen's rejection operated as a powerful force in maintaining the downward trajectory of deportees' identity and mobility. The rationale among countrymen was that return migrants who failed economically abroad had not only failed personally to achieve the central theme in West Indian migration—achievement of social and economic mobility (Bennett 2002)—but had failed the Jamaican society which needed remittances from immigrants.

CHAPTER FIVE
Conclusion

The primary purpose of this book is to look at return migrants from the U.S. and the U.K. and explain how colonial capital at the time of migration affects migration and return migration experiences in home societies where migrants are already indistinguishable by race.

Although the modest sample size does not permit generalization, the results generated in Chapter Two suggest that there were at least two categories of voluntary return migrants. The larger category was made up of returnees from England. They left Jamaica with mid-colonial capital, had little or no financial help from their parents, and focused their activities on attempting to gain mobility out of poverty in Jamaica. Abroad they faced prejudice about their colonial capital and had to postpone their initial 5 years return plan to 30 to 40 years. While abroad for these many years they experienced shifts in habits which affected how they were later identified in Jamaica. Faced with rejection, migrants in this category engaged in transnational activities to ease their disappointment. At times, members of this group who both worked and went to school abroad did identity work to set themselves apart from those who achieved only foreign pensions.

Women and men with mid-colonial capital often felt differently about returning to Jamaica and recast their return migration experiences in light of their occupational experiences abroad.

By and large countrymen had mixed feelings about mid-colonial capital returnees who spent 30 to 40 years abroad to earn full pensions. Countrymen praised their gained wealth, but felt these returnees were still lower class social misfits with money and foreign accents who added to already overpopulated areas, threatened the job security of countrymen; caused crime and violence to increase; and, contributed to inequality by building unnecessary luxury homes merely to establish their economic superiority over poor Jamaicans. Even the civility of this category of returnee was quietly seen by countrymen as odd foreign habits which were out of sync with emerging shifts in Jamaican life.

The high regard that returnees who remained abroad to earn full pensions held about their financial gains was also contravened by coterminous shifts in financial mobility among countrymen. These shifts forced returnees to compete with countrymen by building bigger luxury homes than the many large homes which were built by countrymen who had not migrated.

In the second category of voluntary return migrants were those who left Jamaica with high-colonial capital and enough resources to earn the respect of countrymen and natives in host societies. These migrants focused on attending school, while their parents performed the major income producing economic activities. In addition, their parents and relatives supported them abroad financially. High–colonial capital migrants displayed little or no shifts in their personal habits, and on returning to Jamaica they easily re-negotiated entry into Jamaican society by holding jobs, and owning private businesses.

In Chapter Four when both categories of voluntary return migrants, and deportee return migrants were compared, the extremely low colonial capital of deportees, their youthful age, lack of parental support, and deviant activities took on much significance. Voluntary return migrants of mid- and high-colonial capital tended to leave Jamaica as first generations migrants who maintained their Jamaican work ethic and intestinal fortitude to survive the structural racism which made them invisible ethnically, but visible racially as black and of inferior social status. Some voluntary return migrants pursued higher education and work and others worked full-time in low wage labor jobs—but all pursued a better life by emulating the dominant part of the foreign society they lived in, earned pensions and saved paltry sums while honoring the payment of household bills. This lends support to scholars (e.g., Waldinger 1996) who attribute first generation West Indian success to their willingness to take unwanted jobs, and live on less while delaying luxuries.

In contrast, deportees tended to be 1.5 generation migrants who had too little colonial capital to overcome any bottleneck in opportunities (Portes et al. 1993). Abroad they adopted the ways of their native born peers who did not place high value on higher education, and working in traditional jobs that would eventually pay a pension. Male deportees felt pressured into filling the economic gaps left by their fathers and did not realize that their parents worked for paltry sums to honor their bills. Faced with doubts about their success abroad, deportees took matters into their own hands. They took a sharp turn to a new path often involving petty drug dealing which escalated into criminal activity to meet situational needs. Eventually by force of international law, deportees were stigmatized as criminals, and were denied all opportunity to construct their return path.

Very often mid-colonial capital migrants who spent 30 to 40 years abroad and deportee migrants returned home to attenuated familial and community bonds (Bodnar 1985, Mahler 1995, Wierzbicki 2004). Although these returnees and Jamaican countrymen had common ethnic identity, unfortunately they rejected the shifts in each other's lives. In response to these difficulties, mid-colonial capital returnees who remained abroad 30 to 40 years constructed returned residents associations and transnational lives between different countries. But, deportees could not escape the daily brunt of countrymen's rejection, and stigmatization as transnational criminals. Deportees who had the least colonial capital were homeless, suffered most from alienation, and denial of re-entry into Jamaican communities, as the building of luxury houses was an integral rite of passage. Those deportees who returned to live in family homes and had skills still suffered rejection from the community because they had not built their own homes to meet social expectations associated with migration.

The sharp downward shift in mobility that 1.5 generation migrants experienced (Portes et al.1990) ended in deportation which destroyed their possibility of achieving economic mobility in the U.S. and the U.K. and from participating in transnationalism or negotiating re-entry into Jamaican society. This realization made deportees feel as if their lives would have been better off never having left Jamaica. Their view of Jamaica was not as sweet as the other two categories of returned migrants who had more crucial elements of colonial capital—money, social graces and education. To a certain degree the comparison of migrants with different colonial capital supports claims made in current research (Portes et al. 1993; Waldinger 2006) about inner city segmented assimilation and the transforming effect that life in the U.S. can have on some immigrants.

More importantly, this research helps to clarify migration literature and tempers overly zealous attribution of transnational explanations in the study of migration. In the case of interviewed West Indian migrants, Transnational Theory only applies to migrants with mid-colonial capital who improved their financial capital abroad. Transnational Theory disregards deportees and high-colonial capital migrants. Currently, return migration theories (e.g. NCE, NECL, Structuralism and Transnational Theory) apply only to voluntary return migrants. Hence, there is demand for new theories to apply when immigrants are deported and prohibited by force of law from carrying out the presumed cycle of arrival and departure in similar fashion to voluntary return migrants. To construct a more comprehensive theoretical explanation of return migration experiences I argue that, migration and return migration outcomes are best explained by migrants' colonial capital at the time of migration. The new theory being proposed—Colonial Capital Theory of Migration (CTM) states that, migration and return migration experiences are as complex and varied as one might expect, given migrants' pre-migration colonial capital, and associated shifts in cultural values and economic mobility experienced in host societies

In my research, the effects of colonial capital were robust, as in each society to which migrants moved, they faced ancient prejudices about their colonial capital (education, skin tone, financial capital, family and social graces). Theoretically, in the case of voluntary returning migrants who remained abroad 30 to 40 years to earn full pensions, their colonial capital shared a positive relationship, with declining effect, on their migration and return migration experiences. That is, their bi-focal transnational identity and the transfer of financial capital helped them at first to gain limited entry into foreign societies and Jamaican society. But, they were denied full acceptance because of the ancient prejudices held about other important elements of colonial capital such as lighter skin, formal education, and social graces.

In essence their money did not buy everything. This sociological reality, lead some mid-colonial capital migrants to take the next best action, and marry lighter skinned women. Clearly such action could not improve the personal colonial capital of these migrants, but at least they made some attempt to improve this element for their children. I was surprised that even if this category of returnee improved their education, in the eyes of countrymen, they still did not improve their social graces; even after migrants adopted foreign accents and modes of dress.

High-colonial capital at the time of migration (good education, family support and acquisition of social graces) shared a positive relationship with good migration, and return migration experiences. Abroad, migrants in this category suffered little or no shift in their identity, but achieved educational and financial mobility in 7 to 15 years. On returning to Jamaica, they quickly resettled without being involved in transnationalism. In contrast to both categories of voluntary return migrants, the extremely low colonial capital of deportees shared a negative relationship with migration and return migration. Absent any improvements to even their financial capital, while abroad, returning migration only exacerbated their predicament. In essence, deportees were vulnerable to sharp declines in mobility and identity as they lacked the necessary initial education, family support and social graces to help them achieve socio-economic mobility in home or host countries.

Based on this data there is room for further research exploring the third generation children of voluntary returnees with different colonial capital, and the offspring of deportees who are born abroad. Current scholarship argues that by the third generation, children want to find out about their parent's country of origin, and may return to their parent's homeland. The involvement of children was a major concern for Reg who wished for his children to return to Jamaica and participate in returned residents association activities. In Victor's case he was disappointed that the children he left behind in England did not return to Jamaica after completing university. From the hints returnees gave, their second generation children face an identity crisis. For instance, parents reported that their children when asked if they were English, answered, "I am not English." But, there was no positive identification of themselves as Jamaicans either.

Whatever direction migration research takes, it is hoped that this work helps to inform its readers about how migration can fall apart for different categories of migrants and that colonial capital at the time of migration is useful in constructing adequate migration and return migration theories, and is a predictor of migrants' lives abroad and on returning home; even if they return 30 to 40 years later.

APPENDIX I
Initial Interview Question Guide

To create the initial questions, I followed the example set by Spradley (1979) and, field researchers who interviewed West Indian migrants about their experiences with race in foreign countries (Waters 1999; Vickerman 1999).

The first questions were "grand tour questions"—constructed to get general information. In the actual interviews I then moved to more specific open ended questions about returnees own life experiences and how they negotiated life in Jamaica and abroad. The responses of returned migrants came easily, but clearly with a somber tone which made me live, albeit it for a few moments, their heartfelt experiences which came from enduring years of social exclusion, racism, poverty, extreme cold and health problems.

Date of Interview: _____

Level of formal education: _____

Age: _____

Sex: _____

Place of Birth: Parish _____ Town _____ Country_____

Year when migrated: _____

From which parish: _____

Migrated to: Country _____ City_____

Date of return to Jamaica: _____

Current residence in Jamaica: Parish_____ Town_____

Research Question 1
Having returned to Jamaica where race is not a strong determinant of identity and success, do return migrants re-melt into Jamaican society to become successful? Do they create social boundaries, or experience inhibiting crosscurrent challenges related to having migrated and identified ethnically as black, and inferior?

Interview Questions
- Describe your experiences while living abroad.
- Describe your experiences since returning to Jamaica.
- Describe your experiences over the course of a typical day in Jamaica.
- In what ways are your experiences abroad similar to your experiences in Jamaica?
- In what ways do your experiences abroad differ from your experiences in Jamaica?
- Give examples of any obstacles you have faced since returning to Jamaica.
- Describe the steps you have taken to overcome any obstacles.
- Give examples of success you have had since returning to Jamaica.
- Describe what you have done in Jamaica to achieve/maintain your success.
- Identify the ways in which your experiences abroad prepared you for returning to Jamaica?
- Identify some of your biggest surprises on moving abroad and also on returning to Jamaica?

- Give examples of the ways you were identified by others abroad, and which identity you accepted?
    1. Explain the meaning of your abroad identity choice.
    2. Describe how others identify you in Jamaica?
    3. Explain the meaning of how others identify you in Jamaica.
    4. Compare your experiences abroad with your Jamaican experience.
    5. Give examples of the ways in which being identified as a returned resident helps or hinders you in Jamaica?
- Identify what is important to you in housing.

Research Question 2
What are the categories of Jamaican return migrants and do their contributions relate to their length of stay abroad?

Interview Questions
- Give examples of different types of return migrants?
- Give your reasons for returning to Jamaica?
- Identify your work skills/degree acquired abroad.
- Describe your work involvement in Jamaica on return; if any.
- Do you run/own a private business?
- Are you in full retirement?
- Identify your biggest contribution to Jamaica since returning.
- What do other migrants say about their return to Jamaica?
- In what ways has returning been surprising—both good and bad?
- Describe the social services you had access to while living abroad.
- Identify the social services that are available to you in Jamaica?
- Describe health care in Jamaica and your health needs.
- Describe crime in Jamaica and how it impacts you.

Research Question 3
How do countrymen see Jamaican return migrants?
Interview Questions
- Give examples of ways to identify different types of migrants?
- Identify the physical items that are a must for return migrants to have.
- Describe the relationship between returning Jamaican migrants and resident Jamaicans.
- Are returnees truly Jamaican?
- In what ways have the identity of returnees changed?

APPENDIX II
Full Life Stories for the Curious

This appendix provides the reader with unabridged life stories from deportees, and voluntary return migrants with mid-, and high-colonial capital.

Samuel: A deportee's Life Story
    I was born in Spaldings Clarendon on the 22nd of September 1974. My mother ran a bar and my father drove a Desnoes and Geddes delivery liquor truck, but I lived with my grandmother who ran a restaurant. I was the first child with 2 brothers and 2 sisters. Growing up I went to Spalding Primary School from grades 1 to 5. I then left Spaldings to live with my father and his wife in May Pen. There I finished grade 6 at Hazard Primary, but I did not pass the Common Entrance (a high school entry examination) and so after Hazard Primary went to an All Age school where I passed the Grade Nine Achievement Test to Vere Technical High School. Technical school provided a lot of sports activity such as running and football.
    In 1985 or 86 my mother and her sisters left for the U.S. Her children and my cousins were left with grandma. But the many children were too much pressure for grandma who also ran a restaurant. I was sent to live with my father in May Pen, Clarendon. Going to live with father gave her relief, but I still came home to grandma on holidays and every chance I got. In the US my mother went to school and worked in nursing homes. She landed in Florida with her father but went to work in New York (NY) where friends and family put her on her feet. I hoped that my mother would achieve a better life in the land of opportunity where jobs paid much better. While there she sent home things we did not have things like view masters, bicycles—everything others did not have. She came home every year, even if Christmas was missed she came around Reggae Sunsplash time. I remember good family days, trips to Boston in Portland, and trips to St. Elizabeth with family from abroad.
    I went abroad on the 12th of December, 1992 when mom sent the visa—she did everything herself. Only small things like getting medical tests were

done by family members. All 4 children went abroad together to New York, just as how my mother and her sisters went together—so we went together. On landing in New York I can remember the snow. I remember stopping at KFC, driving in the snow flurries and seeing a friend from Jamaica who had just migrated. It was a good feeling when people who knew us came to visit. Since my mother worked all day these friends took us to the mall, bought us clothes and got us prepared. I saw my mother at night. My school was nearby—in walking distance, but my brother took the bus to his school.

We lived in a nice area called Eden Wall at Dier Avenue and close to the Eden Falls in Bay Chester. Our landlord was Jamaican and lots of other Jamaicans lived nearby. There were West Indian stores and fish shops in the community.

I started to work immediately in New York. In December I did some work with a friend pulling carpet out of a house and used the money to buy nice sneakers and clothes. By January 1993 I started making marijuana deliveries for some Twelve Tribe Rastafarians who owned a fish shop on Bay Chester Road. I went in there regularly to buy Jamaican food and fish tea—since my mother was always working I cooked for myself. The Rastas respected me and always invited me in deeper and deeper. Even if they just saw you 4 days ago they still said "how come you nuh come check the I." They showed videos and kept dances, and they reasoned about the old days in Kingston and Africa. This was a turning point as the Rastas taught me things I needed to know as a man—about the Great Pyramids, that blacks constructed them. A pure big things they dealt with, they respected the philosophy of Marcus Garvey, loved money, sent all of their children to college, and drove Mercedes Benzes. They still respect me and come to see me in Jamaica. They can come and ask for me any time—my family is well known—they can find me without any phone.

This was a turning point, as I started to grow my hair. I always wanted to grow my hair, even when I lived in Jamaica I spent much time with a Rastafarian friend who had a sound system, and a restaurant. They were like my second home and I still call the man father. I have always been around Rastas and it was not strange to be working among them in the US.

In 1993 to 1994, I attended middle school. It was not like Jamaica even though lots of Jamaican attended; it was different. We did not wear uniforms which made it difficult to determine if we were going to school or work. School children drove their own vehicles and even drove stolen vehicles to school, smoked, drank liquor and carried guns. And there were pronounced gangs from Haiti, Puerto Rico. There we had to unite to survive—by myself I was an outcast. Many days, when I arrived at school stood and wondered if I should enter the building or go walking because I did not know anybody. I felt out of place as every class I had to tell my name. There wasn't anything enticing to make me want to go to school. I saw people who wanted to talk to me but conversations were casual. Most people were Jamaican but I did not have a connection with them.

My outsider feelings lasted for about 2 weeks, and Christmas 1993 was nice. I now had a girlfriend and brethren who lived in the basement of my apartment building had a little sound system. I kept a basement party and invited friends from school for food and liquor. My mother and I paid for the food since she liked to cook food for friends. It was a joy for her to hear that I was keeping a party. This made me popular among Jamaicans. My mind strayed from school and after a while felt like I was missing something. I felt like I wanted to go to the street to work and not ask my mother for money. I did not want to be caught up in one place every day. January 1994 I stopped going to school and started selling beef patties and marijuana in a little hole in the wall store owned by Boy. This store was located across from the Eden Hall projects where the 12 year olds residents smoked weed hard, and drank 40 ounce beer. The project buildings were tall and housed a lot of people. Boy became wealthy from this venture, and I bought my first Honda motor car. I also moved out of my mother's house to live in Mt Vernon with a friend from May Pen Jamaica who had a nice house with space. In Jamaica I did not talk with them so much, but saw them wearing their big chains. I reconnected with them at Boy's shop. My mother was easy going and did not say much. She did what made us happy.

I made money to buy things I did not have before and gave people money —my mother did not have to cry about rent. She was not short of any money. Many weeks I left Philadelphia and went to NY to give my mother money. I also sent money home to my half brothers in May Pen.

I was arrested for the first time in the summer of 1994. I usually buzzed people into the store, but on this day I refused to let someone in that looked strange—it turned out to be the narcotics police. After refusing to let in the stranger, he went away and came back with other people in a big van and with a ram rod. They searched the store and found a few bags of weed, but did not find the main stash in food cans.

I was bailed by Boy who was not arrested because he never remained in the store. Boy had many marijuana stores like this over Brooklyn on the Puerto Rico side of town. He had people at his disposal to do what he wanted and money piled up in boxes. After being bailed I went back to the store the same day after I went home and had a bath. A few weeks later we were busted again. To reduce the heat employees were switched between stores—I went to work now at a Dollar Store owned by Boy.

By the end of 1994 I stopped working with Boy because I was tired of being arrested—I was arrested about 3 to 4 times over summer. I came to Jamaica in the summer of 1994 for my cousins wedding. When I went back to New York I started playing DJ music with my basement friend. We played every Saturday and Monday nights at the Crystals Club on White Planes Road— where the #7 train stops. My income was now smaller than when I sold marijuana as I had to hire employees. I had lost my car because due to a crash, and I had to be taking taxis to work. I was always working for myself by keeping my own house parties and dances, and taking pictures of people who came to the clubs.

In December 1994 I took a second job working with Hippo Party to set up chairs for special events, anniversaries and birthdays. I now had a different set of friends who were robbers, thieves and gangsters—bottom of the barrel type of Jamaican people. I hung out with them daily, robbing people. We targeted other Jamaica gangsters from the Shower Posse days who were hit men. I still lived with Boy as I knew him from Jamaica as a Don. He would not disrespect me as I knew him as a big Don in Jamaica and as a smaller Don in Jamaica. I still did business with him, selling weed and I sent people who need weed to him and made marijuana deals for him. He still made money from having me around.

I was arrested when another Jamaica pointed me out to the police as the person who robbed and kidnapped him. I did not kidnap him, my friends did, but I went to the house where he was held. I stayed in jail for 1 week until my mother bailed me out. She did not say anything harsh as she did not know the real story. Her heart was broken and even now in 2006 she still talks about it. Right now I need a little money to build a house but when I asked her, she said, "When you could have made money you ran up and down with friends."

After coming out of jail I went to live with my first baby mother close to Mt. Vernon. I met her one night while walking home. Also I started going to court every few months but the kidnapping case was postponed for many months into 1996.

In 1996 while my kidnapping was being processed I moved to Ft Lauderdale Florida to escape sentencing. I was sick of NY and went to live with my aunt. I left my baby mother with my mother in NY. I started working with my uncle in Lee Building Construction Company. My uncle was a big man there who sorted out building specs. I made good money from construction work and helped to build many big houses. I also sold weed and knew the business from Boy who had links in Florida. I even recommended my brother to Boy. I sent money home to needy relatives. I met a Jamaican woman in Florida who owned a restaurant and started hanging out all night at the restaurant and selling weed from the tail gate of my truck in front of the restaurant. This new girl from the restaurant became pregnant around this time (I later married her). I moved from my aunt after 3 to 4 months after I met my girlfriend. I also bought a car and looked like I lived in Florida for many years. I passed people who I came and saw walking. After a while I stopped going to construction work daily but went when I wanted a big money. Florida was not an easy heat to work in, but I give thanks for my many years there because now I can tie one hand behind my back and lay blocks all day, tie steel, and build anything. I built my own steps at my house here in Jamaica. After being deported I came and saw pure mud but I built steps all around. Construction helps me to make money in Jamaica. It's hard work but I can see a JA$10,000 in my hand after work—I see solid money in my hand when I work construction. I can buy 3, or 4 pairs of shoes, and give my woman any money.

At the end of 1996 I joined a Pardner in Florida which had a US$100 per week hand. The draw was about US$3,000. I used this money to build my own sound system. I now had enough resources to move my mother, brother, and baby mother down to Florida. My mother worked in cook shops. My oldest sister went to school and my brother fixed up the sound and took care of my needs. I worked with him and I gave him a car or anything he needed.

In 1997 my sound was playing all over Florida, at different clubs, and at many more pool parties than in New York. My family knew people and my girl friend's restaurant knew people. People knew my sound in Ft Lauderdale. My brother told me about the profits that we could make from cars in Jamaica and so I wanted more money to buy 2 cars to run taxi cabs in Jamaica. I knew I could earn this money by making weed runs like I did when working for Boy. I then went to Texas and started shipping drugs to New York on trucks owned by Jamaicans. This lasted for all of 1997. I bought a house in Coral Springs Florida, cars for my brothers, girlfriend, and mother. My girlfriend started to work at a car dealership and she helped everybody in the family to own cars. When you are centrally based as a Jamaican you get a lot of news, and this was the Jamaican circle in Florida. The motto was if the information applies, hitch on—if it does not apply, then let it fly. I linked with Boy's friends and that was the Jamaican circle—it was a tight circle excluding Haitians and others. I opened up a new weed supply door to Haitians and Puerto Ricans from Florida, Texas and New York—but even though they might buy from you, they did not get too deep with you.

I now began to experience a rough life, but I could not go back to Jamaica because of the kidnapping case—my workers got robbed, arrested, beaten-up by the supplier, or workers robbed me by giving in less money than the amount of drugs given. Sometimes I had to run leaving my car.

In 1998 I moved back to NY by myself. My brother in Florida sent the weed to NY where I sold it from a friend's barber shop. Everything was now going back to pay living expenses for my second child and relatives. I did not have anybody around to guide me. I had a lot of girlfriends and was supplying other people's needs. I lost my old friends and linked up with new people. In the middle of the year, I went to Florida for a month and kept parties for about a month. It was as if I knew I was going to jail—that was what my friends said. In the summer of 1998 I went back to NY as my new girlfriend in New York said I should come back. She was a school teacher who was older than my mother—she now has a stroke but has come many times to see me in Jamaica.

Unfortunately, while in NY, one day I was smoking a joint in a park and was arrested for possession. The old 1996 kidnapping warrant came up and I could not get bail—I stayed in jail from then until my deportation in 2002. After receiving a 4 1/2 year sentence I first went to Riker's Island for 3 months, and then to Cape Vincent prison on the border of Canada and the US—near to Lake Ontario.

This was another TURNING POINT—I described one with the Rastas and I am describing another one. Everyone's life has several turning points. I did not know that so many prisons existed and so many people who looked like me were imprisoned. The State determines your condition, when blacks live in a dilapidated State, their state is also dilapidated. I realized how many blacks lived their lives in jail. I learned about a new morality and that there was an unseen hand which worked against a nation and a people. Prison was an awakening to see the crisis of a people who looked like me. On the street I did not associate with African Americans. The only African American I associated was my school teacher girlfriend, and she was an intellectual.

In jail I took up things that were helpful to me, I took up construction classes and I also got a GED. I already knew what they taught me about construction but went along for the certificates. The only new things I learnt was how to lay bricks and make fireplaces. I also worked in the kitchen and that has helped me to build a restaurant in front of my house in Jamaica. In prison I also volunteered as a person to clean up blood. I linked up with artists, Muslims from the Nation of Islam and Five Percenters—similar to when I linked up with the Rastas. I realized that trouble was what got me in jail and so I did positive things. During my imprisonment the only thing I was caught with was dirty urine from smoking too much marijuana. They never caught me when I beat boys, and cut some up.

I started a Jamaican football club in prison. We had to fight to get the goals and balls. We noticed that other groups had stuff and formed our own copy cat organization to get out of the dorms. We also made special requests to staff to see special videos about Mandela and Africa.

In the jail the whites were racist. In Cape Vincent there was one black who called himself a French Canadian. But from the moment they saw that I was not causing trouble they worked with me. I became a foundation and a rock. Someone could come to say they were having a problem and I could easily send someone to go tell them to not trouble this Jamaican. I could even send someone to cut them up with can tops. I still had people on the street sending marijuana money and this made me worse, as I created my own world. My family still came to see me and even sent strangers to come check me. A brethren even sent girls to come check me with marijuana. On visitation days I felt them up as if I knew them for a long time.

To serve my sentence I went to 3 different jails and in each I did the same thing, I lived, wrote letters, got packages, and telephoned people. I always said time is longer than rope and I will soon go home.

At Cape Vincent I received many court hearing dates, I did not fight deportation because I did not see the US as my life and blood. I told them to send me home, as I knew that I could live better here in Jamaica. I had my skills, my two hands and my health. I did not have toothache or any sickness. I told them to send me home voluntarily—I did not fight them nor want them to do a lot of paper work. I was willing to pay for my own fare as I did not want to spend another December in jail.

In route to being deported I was sent from Cape Vincent to Water Town jail and then to Ulcer County Jail. I was in solitary all the way as they did not want deportees to steal other inmates' stuff. I then went to Pike Country Jail where people were held for INS services. It was a transit point with many computers. I did not like Pike as it was a racist place and I did not see any black there. At Pike, Jamaica prisoners made trouble to leave, masked up the TV, and refused to eat their bad macaroni, chicken nuggets and fish. We wanted to go to a place where there was a good facility with a exercise yard and free telephones. At each deportation station our families had to pay for collect telephone calls. I could have shown my Jamaican bad self but did not. The places did not make me feel like I wanted to stay.

I don't remember the last jail as I traveled alone all the time in a big car from jail to jail. On the day that I was deported two officers came and got me; one was black and the other was white. They told me that they did not expect any trouble out of me and that I would be able to call my family from the airport. On arriving at the airport in Washington, DC I called my relatives in Jamaica who told me my mother would be returning from a funeral in Jamaica to the US on that same day. My relatives said, "Don't worry yourself we will send a car for you."

On the airplane, I went freely from seat to seat and looked down on Cuba from the airplane window. On arriving in Jamaica I was not questioned by the police. I stayed with my sister in St Burg until I found a place of my own from the US$1000 I had saved. I lived well in jail and that is why I had so little money. I lived in St. Burg until 2003 and earned money by making video tapes of important events, playing my sound and keeping parties. I moved back to live with Grandma taking her to hospital in a wheel chair to get her toe and then her foot cut off. I stayed with her all through this, I even have a video with her in the hospital.

As a deportee there are different looks people have given me. Some expect more than love and joy—they expect sneakers. I am a gangster who knows how to run these types of people from around me. But there are genuine people who still come around who love you for you. Those who say I make Jamaica look bad, I run them off. I don't want to be average, or use my criminal skills to hurt people. I know deportees in the Jamaican street who can come across the barriers in Jamaica and tear people's skins. I currently live in Grandma's house and am building one for myself. I do any trade to survive, like string a house, build things out of wood and I started selling weed just like abroad. The police have come to bust me and they have shot after me, but I just go behind the house and wait till they leave.

After my final arrest in the US I did not lose anything, as my wife sold the house in Florida and I still have my sound in Jamaica. Due to the help I get from my wife, mother, brothers that is where I set my financial limits. I don't just sit around and look for handout. I go and look for work too from the owners of new building projects.

I can tell you I was in jail with some dangerous people who have been deported and from the pattern of the crimes committed in Jamaica, can tell which deportee committed it. A lot of deportees are around and will not go hungry. I do not want to be like them and drag others down. I want to move out on my own.

I always maintained contact with my father and saw him a few months ago. I did not write my people in Jamaica from jail—my wife made those contacts-because I know how Babylon works and I don't give them more information than they need. Just knowing how to deal with a Jamaican is fundamental. Jamaicans are quick to love but they take time to hate you. Never let a Jamaican feel like you are using them, let them feel like they are helping you. Just being around people daily I learned to not drive down people. I live easy, as people realize that I have sense and knowledge. I read many books in jail to build my mind about the planets, and the oceans. I did not limit myself.

You can initiate certain things with words—they are power and can be used to gain influence. Psychological games are played everyday and unseen ideas are used to govern people and nations. I use this on the Jamaican street to live better than people who have more time and energy than I. Sometimes I don't have any money and I just make some badges and sell them. I photocopy the picture and make about 300 to 400 badges. Some deportees will go hungry, but I know that I can go make photocopies of pictures, glue on the picture and sell it. I live off of my knowledge. I don't beg money, instead I give away money, clothes and sneakers, and give away food from my cook shop.

I built my cook shop from zinc blown off of this shop, termite wood and old blocks. I do not live off of criminalization activities, as a deportee I can do that easily. I even have a farm that supplies Pop Chow—I do everything to survive. In all of my trial and tribulation I tried to build up people, not to hurt or tease people to make them cry. That is the way I lived as a youth, and even in jail. I helped people to fix their problems. If I pass you broken down I will help you and you don't have to pay me. I use my mind and instinct to look at life. The other day my nephew came to me and said, "that boy kicked me," I held back the bully and let my nephew kick him. I am a people person who grew up in a family setting. I don't like sadness. I like celebrating birthdays. People make the world.

I like things—like Malcolm X said, "by any means necessary." Why sit in the back of the bus when you can sit in the front. Make civil disobedience to make a point like Gandhi. I try to look for different things in these modern times, and like the US don't just destroy things, but destroy things to make them better—like they destroyed Iraq to make things better.

Being in Jamaica I don't take back the same ways that sent me to jail. The influx of deportees has hurt the country, and psychological damage has been done by saying deportees are responsible for crimes. I do positive things to overcome this emphasis in the news about deportees. If you hear a news report it will always say that a deportee and a man were fighting. It is not just a man and a man was fighting. I try to build myself to overcome the stigma of fear, and mistrust people have of deportees.

Olivive: A Female Deportee's Life Story

I was born on November 17, 1955 at the Montego Bay General Hospital in the parish of St. James. As I remember my first residence at the age of three was then Glen Devon Road—there was a row of houses perched on a broad hill, and a paved main road was at the bottom—our house was the last on the right. The homes were built back to back, meaning the front of each building faced the road and the back faced empty land space and another road. It was in this house the third child in the family died—he would cry constantly and his tummy was hard, and something seemed to bother his head, or so I thought. The funeral service was held at the bottom of the hill near the road. He had spent his last days at the home covered under his mosquito net with a saucer of salt placed over his navel—he was buried in a small area on a friend's land overlooking a not so deep ravine. I dreamt I saw him levitating above his grave and told my father he was not dead, so they should go for him. Of course Dad visited the burial site and told me he was alright.

Well, in coming months the family packed up and left with three children in a little four door Morris and relocated residence on Whitehall Terrace Road off Red Hills Road where my parents had bought land and built a shop. My mother was a floor sales clerk in Kingston and my father was a tile maker at Crichton Brothers. We used a part of the shop and rented out the rest. For one year we did a Patty and Cocoa-bread business.

Those days they had Black-heart men driving round in big long black cars. Once I think I was almost a victim, but just before I reached the vehicle I saw my father coming, he called out to me and grabbed my hand as if to say —she is mine, no. During that same year my grandmother became ill with the shingles and had to come and stay with us. When my father's father died, we all packed up and went to St. Elizabeth for the funeral, which we did not get to attend, because upon our arrival just before dawn we saw them placing the last dirt on the mound—so I never knew what any of my grandfathers looked like. But, I heard they were both very dark featured men, my mother's father was short, and my father's daddy was tall.

At the age of five a brother of my father migrated to the U.S.A. He had a son who was stolen by my mother on our trip to grandfather's burial. He was a very pleasant and proud boy who loved my father with all his little heart. Whenever he and his father visited us in Kingston he would run to his father saying, "Si mi Papa, a fi mi Papa dis." This was because he called both my father, and his father Papa. But he always remembered his father and announced his coming as "Si me Papa." I will never forget his little face as he ran to greet him—he knew him on sight. Eventually, his father took him back from St. Elizabeth because he cried for his father a lot. Well, I loved his father as much as he did, and the next time I saw him we were residing on Mauberly Avenue, and about to leave for the U.S.— that morning I lost a tooth that never grew back. It was at Mauberly Avenue that I experienced my first sexual contact with the boy next door. He was a little man, the eldest of three as it was in my family also. He came over one day and washed and scoured the pots for me and then took me into the bathroom which was adjacent or part of the whole building itself and put his hard little penis in my panties and told me we were married. Of course I was appalled, but said nothing. We would stand at the fence in the evenings and talk and look at each other and then one day he came and did the penis panty thing again, this time outside the fence. Trust me, I was becoming aroused when my visiting grandmother stepped from the house and called me. We were caught and two nights later both of us got the beating of our natural lives. They beat us and said we were not to be seen talking at the fence anymore. I think it was at this residence my family's fifth child was born. She was the first child to be sickly with whooping cough, chicken pox, and measles. Oh gee she was very sickly, and so the family relocated once more to a much larger residence with indoor bathroom and kitchen—at the old house we went outside to use the kitchen and bathroom. In the new residence it was just a case of leaving one room to another—no going outside to the kitchen or bathroom and now there were two big bedrooms, a dining area and a large hall in which we did our playing. It was at this residence my mother gave me the girl talk—I was eight years old. It was 1962, and I lived on the same street with Prince Buster who sang, "If you live in a glass house don't throw stones." The first time I actually saw him, he looked simple enough. I guess there wasn't any stage garb on him when he was at home. That year I enrolled in my first public school—Half Way Tree Primary—I started in Grade 2B, and that B followed me through primary school to Papine Junior High and to the eight grade. I was then transferred to 8A then 9A, where I graduated in 1972. That year or the next we relocated again, and it was at this residence that I suddenly woke up hearing my father telling an old ragged molester to leave the neighborhood and never return because he would kill him. The molester would sit at the gate and try to converse with the neighborhood children who usually threw things at him and teased him. Myself and my brother and sisters were never a part of that group because we felt it was bad manners, and besides that we were cautioned to not do as other children did. But he was not trustworthy, one day he visited our home to see my father who was trying to find work for him and tried to stick his fingers in my panty—he wanted to see if I still had my hymen. My parents were in the living room and saw him. That year the youngest of the living five was born, and we were now a family of eight—five children, mother, father, and a live-in helper who had been with us since 1962. She was a disabled orphan who had worked for our grandaunt-in-law who was a matron at the Kingston Public Hospital. Mother, as she was fondly named, was married to my father's uncle. During all our relocations my mother's mother always visited, brought fruits of the season, cook dinner and baked.

My father migrated to the U.S. when I was age 9, I don't know where in the U.S. he went because my mother and father were tight-lipped. Then my mother migrated leaving us with the household helper and my grandmother who came from Montego Bay to visit. I heard that the helper was committed to us because she suffered from polio and had no family. She taught us math, English, and good manners, and reinforced the good qualities that my parents started. My parents were good providers and sent money every Thursday without fail. Sometimes the helper sent me to change the currency. Our rent was paid from a different source, other than the money my parents sent but food money came out of the weekly mail.

My parents were gone for 4 years before they received our visas. After 2 years they might have visited us in Jamaica. All of the children went abroad in

March of 1972 but not me. I had an accident with a passenger bus belonging to the Jamaica Omni bus Service, and from January 1972 to July 1972 I was on the orthopedic ward at University of the West Indies Hospital. On January 25th I was walking along Molynes Road in route to the passport office to replace my damaged passport and talking with my brother about a romantic breakup with a prominent Jamaican race horse jockey. Just past a bus shed I heard someone shout look out! I turned to find myself face to face with a bus which hit my right shoulder. I fell and looked to see the tires moving towards my legs. I pulled my right leg away thinking that could roll to my left, like in the James Bond movies, to avoid my left leg being run over. Unfortunately, as I rolled the bus broke my left ankle and dislodged my hip. The helper still took care of me and my father came to Jamaica with an extension for my visa. I was happy to be going abroad and looked forward to the new things that could happen in my life. On arrival in the U.S., I planned to become an airline stewardess which would fund my way through medical school.

My father came to meet me at the airport since my mother was at work. She was a nursing assistant in nursing homes. After that job she got a job in a hospital which is what raised us. From the airport I saw tall trees, and smooth roads; not that I did not have smooth roads in Kingston. That's all we had in Kingston. I was surprised to see the small lawns and how close the houses were to the streets. In other respects it resembled Kingston.

My parents lived in the city of Washington, DC itself. The new home was large and nice and my siblings were there waiting along with the rest of the neighborhood. The new home was large and nice, and my siblings were there waiting along with the rest of the neighborhood. The house had 3 stories with a basement that had a little window; this was something new that I never had in Jamaica. The bedrooms were small; I thought so. The verandahs were different in America they were not as low as ours were in Jamaica and Americans called verandahs, porches.

In 1972 I started high school in the 10th grade. I earned an A average for the 1st year, C in my 2nd year and F for my 3rd year. I fitted in school for the 1st year. I was bright, always a reader of *True Confession*, comics, and I was very knowledgeable. Additionally, half of the things I did in the 10th grade I had already done in Jamaica. In my neighborhood for the first two years I did not associate with any Jamaicans. The neighborhood was African American. They were militant about their black power. The neighborhood had a few whites' yards were well manicured, dogs had to be fenced in. Their social outlook was upper middle class, doctors and teachers.

In my second year of puberty I started getting low esteem. I fell short in classes and only worried about getting money and a job. I got a job in the Washington Youth Core Program and did baby sitting jobs. I also had a 2 year scholarship of $500 from the Woodridge Foundation to help replace my teeth with dentures and help with school expenses. In September 1973 I applied for a Student Work Study Program to work in the school. In the summer I worked in the recreational centers in the elementary school; like summer youth camps.

By the 3rd year I decided to stop attending day classes because money from the Woodridge Foundation and summer student work study programs was not enough. One could not get the work study program for 1 year, but still the money was small. I tried going to night school but got kicked out because this young man tried to pick me up and I kissed my teeth. The boy reported me and the head person came and threw me out. He ruined my life. I did not formerly graduate from high school and had a lame leg from the JOS accident. My leg would swell up from an ulcer on the leg. I could not do anything without the high school diploma and my parents said nothing.

1973 was a memorable year as I went to my first all night Jamaica party with a Jamaican girlfriend. We went over to some guy's house that attended Howard University. Nothing happened sexually, but we just crashed from being tired. This was Washington DC in the 1970s they took nothing from anyone. I was use to attending adult parties from the age of 15 in Jamaica and staying out until 4:00 or 5:00 a.m. We went to different parties every weekend. One week it would be Jamaican, the next would be American, then Panamanian, and then Trinidadian. We were integrated ethnically in our social life. There were Africans who came to Howard to do their Ph.D.

On the first night out, my mother told my siblings to lock the doors and I had to wait until 7:00 a.m. when my mother came home. My girlfriend's mother called my mother to get clemency and my mother said, "okay." To avoid getting a beating I just went in got my stuff and went to live with my Jamaican girlfriend for a little while but ended up staying from September to October. If my mother said anything I would move out to my girlfriend and her mother's house. If my girlfriend's mother said anything, I would go home to my mother's house. My father never lived with use from the time we went to the US. This was unusual as this was the same father who would go to meet his wife although she just worked around the corner; he took his children to church, and looked after his children. I don't know what happened. I heard that he and my mother had an argument and he hit her. My daddy claimed that there were too many women in the house and he wasn't going to live with so many women. He still visited or called. He came over in the day time especially if my mother complained to him about our actions.

My sisters' attendance was good until their first year in junior high school when attendance trickled to nothing. The four girls became totally distracted from any academic work and did not graduate from any schools. Only my brother continued his education on an athletic scholarship to a community college in California. He acquired a bachelor's degree in engineering, got married and returned home to Washington, DC with six children.

By 1975 I was introduced to smoking weed by a Panamanian fellow and my girlfriend. My Jamaican girlfriend met this guy who introduced me to his friend. My girlfriend took a tout every now and again and I took a tout too. I started smoking herb, but did not do pills. I was part of a hippie black culture that emphasized that black was for blacks, and black was beautiful. Black students used their student loans to take trips to Africa.

It was a good thing because now we see blacks in good jobs. To achieve this, back then we picked out the good, made known what we wanted, and fought for our justice. We were not just destructive, but were tireless in what we wanted. We adopted the African culture in dress, and recognized African Liberation Day, Malcolm X Park, MLK's birthday. We dressed up to attend the Apollo Theater. Anything to big up blacks we pursued. We were proud of Washington, DC being 95% black; whites lived in Virginia. We stood guard at Howard University to ensure that black students completed their work—if a student needed to use the main frame we would block the doors to make sure that student completed his work.

In 1979 I left home and hitch hiked for one month to visit my brother in California, and hopefully start a new life. Well, one morning I went job hunting and scratched my brother's car, he threw me out and told me to return home because California wasn't a good place for me. The California pace was too fast, so I hitch hiked on tractor trailers home. In route home to DC, I was taken to truck stops in New York, Virginia, and Maryland. I started just traveling with them for fun and adventure but at the end of every year I would go to California. First year I traveled central states and returned southern; the next year I went southern and returned northern.

In 1983 I decided to stay home and pursue my goal of attending DC University. But mom called the cops who sternly told me that I was of age and would be locked up if I returned to my parent's residence, I told the cops that I had no where to go, so they took me to a shelter and dropped me off.

I moved from shelter to shelter in DC until I hitch hiked to Hartford, Connecticut. I had no place to live, and after 7 days the police took me to the Salvation Army in downtown Hartford. I made big strides by going back to high school to earn my GED. Then I got my nurses aid certificates to work in nursing homes because they had stopped using the Red Cross Certificates. Welfare helped me to get an apartment but I mostly stayed at the YMCA where I had access to a television and my own bathroom. This was in 1986 when Reaganomics permitted some people to go back to school. I started attending community college and did general studies in liberal arts to get me up to snuff academically. Then I got a job with the government as a processing clerk in the state library which only lasted only 2 years because of economic recession. After, I got a temporary job with the state troopers with the possibility of getting a permanent position. The troopers did a background check and the police who later came to arrest me said as soon as he punched in my name the computer went wild.

The social services had put out a warrant over the past 4 years claiming that I had defrauded them. I knew who had done this; there was a clerk who felt that I was too smart to be on welfare. I was arrested, charged and bailed all in three hours and lost the newly acquired job as a receptionist for the Connecticut State Troopers. I decided to return to school to finish my degree and learn something about computers

I enrolled in a certificate program that taught the IBM software. It was during this tenure that I became caught up in the real drug/hard drug (crack-cocaine) I started smoking to ease some pressure. I became lethargic and actually fell asleep in every class. I attended classes three twice per week from 10:00 a.m. to 7:30 p.m., this left me three days to study and play. As the case was, I was now an amputee i.e., I had lost my leg in 1992 while I was working at the state library. For 15 years, since 1983 I had developed super glycemia, the symptoms some took as evidence of being on drugs. I found that whenever I ate eggs my heart race, and I fainted. I self treated my condition with diet which is what I now blame for the lethargy.

Anyhow, I was on my way to acquiring an associate degree and that was good enough for me, but I fell along the way. I decided to visit my family in Toronto and tried hitch hiking across the border, but was stopped and sent to the nearest town where I resided for three years. That was when someone introduced me to some young drug dealers who lived next door—they asked me to be their middle person. At first I said no, but then accepted. I was arrested and charged with possession, trafficking, and sale of narcotics and sentenced to one to three years in prison, I did five months in jail and six months in maximum security because of my disability and there was only one prison which had a facility for the handicapped. It took them one year to deport me because I had written to the United Nations, and the Jamaican Consulate in New York, and had applied for a review of my case. The Jamaican Consulate wrote back stating that I had no morals, and they could not do anything for me. After being in the US for twenty- eight years I was deported from the U.S., escorted to an immigration office at the Montego Bay airport where I was interviewed and released. "You are on your own" the officer told me, "You are free to go." That was good, I HATED BEEN LOCKED UP so I walked out of the airport and asked the first Jamaica Union of Taxi Association (JUTA) driver if he knew where I could fi-nd a cheap room to rent? While living in upstate New York I received social security disability payments and after I got locked-up I continued receiving my allowance until I began my sentence at the state prison. This is how I survived the shock I bought my clothes for traveling in, and so on. All my little bit of accouchements I had acquired between 1995 and 1998 were left behind except for the Alien Registration Card. The police informed me that I could send for it belongings and after 5 years some deportees can apply for re-entry to the USA. I walked out of the airport in Mobay and a JUTA driver helped me to find a room on Church St. in Mobay.

From there I began my life as a returning residence with US$150 on hand, and US$800 in my US bank account. Later I wrote my bank and they sent me this sum pronto. Here I was in 2000, age 46, and returning to Jamaica without any formal education or certificates. I had turned down so many short term certificates to acquire something very special in my life that could be of much use to my decorum and my country and now I had returned without anything. Everything was sucked out, but I had no intention of giving up. Jamaicans were not the losing type. It's a joke that we all had 200 jobs in the US. I put on my thinking cap and started out, first thing was to acquire a bank account which to my surprise became a scream, I had to be recommended by someone, just to open an account, and on the form I had to disclose the amount being lodged. Also my US$800 bank check was going to take 45 days to clear. I had to open with someone else meaning my bank account was really in someone else's name, and I was second recipient. I had asked my landlord to be my reference, but I needed two references. He referred me to another Justice of the Peace who in turn helped by lodging my check to his account and give me the money from his funds so I could pay rent and eat.

A young woman offered me a job in her gift and accessories shop. I worked for her for three years until September 2004 when she decided that she could not afford to pay a 2 year retroactive increase in minimum wage, and that she was now powerful enough to meet out physical abuse. I took her to the Department of Labor but the judge said that because the young woman had given me her old clothing, she and I did not have a employer-employee relationship.

Now I was in the streets again because I could not pay my rent and had to give up my room. I asked a male associate of mine to put me up but within 3 nights he threw me out. After trying to locate family here in Mobay, I found out my grandmother my uncle were dead, and the only living relative in Jamaica, could not put me up.

On the streets of Mobay, deportees were fresh catch for every wrong doer in town. They would all be your buddy if you wanted to spread your wings in crime. Not me! I have always been a law abiding citizen and plan to remain so even if I am a drug addict, which I am not. After the friend threw me out, two days later I went to the Parish Council. The story of my life and this one are two different stories. In January 2005 I found myself homeless in Montego Bay and went to the Poor Relief Department of the Parish Council to seek shelter, because I was told prior that the parish does not have a homeless shelter in Albion—so I went seeking somewhere to reside as I put myself back together. This was my second visit, because at the time of the check cashing business, I had reason to seek shelter, but the Parish Council refused to help because I had money. But this time I had no money or anything so after interviewing me, I was sent with a letter to the coordinator to allow me to stay until I could help myself. I was seen by Mr. D who informed me that the shelter was not the kind as I would expect. Well my expectation was not the issue, after trying to spend the night walking the streets for two nights, I found myself surrounded by male predators who would try or do anything to get what they wanted, and that was sex, as I was cornered by two unknown men while standing on the corner of an intersection, I was saved by another but more thoughtful predator—he was an acquaintance who saw my danger and stopped. After explaining my dilemma, he told me to return to the bar and wait for him—he was going to rent a room for me/us—well he took me to his home for the rest of the night which was all of three hours, because he lived far, it was late, and I had to be out before his landlord's early rise which was 5:30 a.m. So by 6:00 a.m. on January 3, 2005, I was walking down Barnett Street with JA$135 for breakfast. I waited until 8:30 a.m. to go to the Municipal building which was on Union Street in Montego Bay. I explained my dilemma to a social worker who took my demographics and told me to wait to see the shelter director. After an interviewing conference, the director decided to allow me to enter the Refuge of Hope Montego Bay Shelter for the Homeless with a written letter of introduction and approval I found my way to the shelter's location by route taxi and a driver who knew its direct location. It was open because it was after 5:00 p.m. Mr. D had explained that it was usually closed between the hours of 8: a.m. to 4:00 p.m. I went in and someone was at the desk situated at the entrance. I handed him my letter, which he read, introduced myself and asked if I need food. I replied, "yes" and he said that supper would be served at 6:00 p.m. He showed me to the ladies dorm and assigned me to a bed and explained the procedures as well as introduced me to the rest of the residents. My first night was comfortable—I took a bath and bedded down—early the next morning we were awakened by the turning on of lights and a woman walking through waking up residents. Persons were becoming fully awake and others that had come in after I had fallen asleep were present. I think I went to sleep at about 7:00 p.m., because I did not want to be drowsy when it was time to get up and go out. There was one person in particular that I recognized because she was a visitor to the first community where I had resided in Mobay, and at the gift shop where I worked—she was in a mental health program which saw to the dispensation of her medication and other daily activities of living. At first I did not speak, but allowed her to introduce herself, I thought she would not have recognized me, but she did. She asked how I was and proceeded to make small talk before reminiscing as to where she had seen me before—I told her. She smiled and conceded, and walked away. I became a resident asking guarded questions every now and then, and doing my thing which was selling mirrors, *Sunday Gleaner* and *Observer,* and minding my own business. Mentally incapacitated persons can be selfishly rebellious at times and these were no different—they carried on as though they were the only type of people that should be at the shelter. But there were residents who were not mentally ill residing there. So therefore, I protect-

ted myself and tried to make acquaintances, but other residents were quiet se-
cretive, watchful and a bit mischievous—they would leave the larger chores
undone or just refused to do any.

I had enrolled myself in a H.E.A.R.T/N.T.A. program and in late January I
was called in to attend an interview—I went and was informed that I was expected to pay a fee, find my own uniform, books, school supplies, as well as
transportation expenses. I panicked, but spoke to my mentor at the *Gleaner*
newspaper company—he helped me with an extra JA$200 to purchase a blouse
and skirt and told me to talk to someone at the Parish Council. Well I went
back to the shelter director who informed me that he could help. I then attended
classes five days per week and did vending on Saturdays and Sundays to pay
for transportation—but sales were bad. Also, I was going to the shelter late, at
7:30 p.m. daily, and this seemed to look as though I was getting special treatment. To avoid being thrown out, I fervently explained to the shelter coordinator that I needed this program to help myself out of the shelter environment. I
then took to doing the female bathroom on a daily basis after I showered at
nights—this they liked. No one wanted to do toilets—the task was beneath their
integrity—but it had to be done. The coordinator said nothing and allowed me
to come in late at night. Every morning we all left together, but other residents
returned first and by the time I returned, they already had supper and were
ready for bed. All was well though, as my social worker started funding my
lunch and transportation and also gave me a monthly allowance of JA$400.
This helped immensely as I had to buy, beg and coerce public health (type V)
clinic to help out with dressings for the ulcer on my residual (stomp).

*Victor: Illustrating Mid-colonial capital Migrants who acquired wealth aboard
and improved their education*

I was born August 1st. 1928 in a little district named Sandy Gutt (near Harewood), St. Catherine in a religious family. My entire mother's fami-
ly/relatives were Anglicans while my father, although he did not attend church
had strong Baptist persuasions, we all looked forward to him leading the family
singspiration on Sunday evenings.

My religious environment including my elementary school which was an
Anglican school are responsible for instilling in me high moral and spiritual
values. The words of philosophy learned at Harewood Elementary School e.g.,
"Heights of great men reached and kept were not attained by sudden flight, but
they while their companions slept were toiling upwards in the night," "Anything worth doing is worth doing well," and "There's always room at the top"
have guided my success through life.

Growing Up Poor

We knew what it meant to be poor. My father was a tailor who always
rented a shop in a neighboring town/village to carry out his trade. One of my
weekly duties was to walk bare footed on unpaved rock-stone roads for at least
twelve miles to and fro in order to collect the family allowance of maybe five
shillings every fortnight.

My mother kept a little "higgler shop" and this was a second major duty—
to help her to run the shop as she suffered from failing eyesight for many years,
so from the age of about eight years she sent me in the company of the higglers
to Coronation Market on the market train on Thursday mornings where I sold
agricultural goods. On Saturday mornings I bought goods for the shop and retu-

rned on the market train Saturday afternoons. I got home just in time to grab a bite and man a stall on the China Man shop piazza at Sandy Gutt on Saturday nights. A high point of all this was that at age eight I knew all the wholesalers in Kingston and which items to buy from whom at the lowest price.

My third major task was to take chocolate (dried cocoa beans) to sell at Cocoa Walk and return with a zinc pan of wet sugar to sell in mom's higgler shop. Carrying this zinc pan of sugar was sheer hell as it weighed about as much as a bag of cement. My neck was pushed down in my shoulder, and at age fifteen I was only about forty inches tall.

Move to Kingston

I moved to Kingston at the age of fifteen years and three days, to live with my elder sister who was settled there. I was apprenticed to R.E.Taylor of 117 Princes St. to learn French polishing for the princely wage was two shillings and six pence per week. After 3 months fire broke out when 2 senior workmen were attempting to cut a rum quart bottle for use as a drinking glass—there was pandemonium all around as flames erupted and 3 three men in flames were screaming and running around the shop. I had flames on my face and shirt, but I remembered what I learned in school, "If your clothes are on fire don't run around, roll on the ground". I did just that, so my injury was minor compared to the others who got burnt, never-the-less I spent three weeks in KPH as a result of being a spectator of a stupid experiment.

When I was discharged from the KPH, I became, "man of the house" as my sister was now in an advanced stage of pregnancy and forsaken by all, including our parents who made arrangements for me to go and live with a distant cousin. I disobeyed my parents' instructions and was also disinherited by them. I just could not desert my sister at a time like this when she had no one else in her corner. The next few months were very challenging; I had to pay the Lying-in fee (maternity fee); when my nephew was born I did all the laundry, cooked her dinner and took it to her as did most the other visitors. I registered my nephew's birth and named him, gave him one of my teacher/mentor's name; Balfour.

I was transferred to the furniture showroom with a increase in pay to five shillings per week but had to earn more to meet all the family's needs. As a result I made handles for straw bags which I sold to the craft vendors in the Coronation Market. This was the mother of innovations as the only tools I had were a compass saw and a gimlet. I finished them with shoe polish as I had no facilities for conventional finishing.

We moved house four times in the next year or so; the last was memorable. We could not afford to hire a hand-cart so we packed all our earthly possessions on our single-bed spring and placed it on our heads, I in front and my sister in the rear. We set out in the beautiful moon light night across the waste lands along the foot-paths linking the neighboring communities. Dogs barked all around; I was afraid but my sister assured me dogs that bark don't bite. In a moment she yelled, "him bite me" I couldn't laugh, but I wished I could have.

We made another move as we could now afford better accommodations. I left R. E. Taylor and was working with Mr. George DaCosta, things were slow I was not earning much. My sister was now working and had a helper taking care of her two children while she was at work. I contributed to the household expenses, but at times when there was no work I had no money, but my sister did not believe me, so she told her helper not to give me anything to eat. I went two full weeks without eating: after the first week I was so weak that I could not get out of bed; I told the other tenants in the yard that I was not feeling well. I could not tell them the truth as my sister, at this time, was better off than all of them. Neither did I tell my parents seeing I had disobeyed their instructions earlier on. To this day I haven't told them. However, when one of the other tenants told my father, he was livid.

Some good came out of this experience as when the facts were known the son of one of the tenants took me to his workplace, Jamaica Fruit and Shipping Company, where I was employed as a mail clerk at twenty five shillings per week. This enabled me get my own room and enjoy a little easier life. I was able to send Regular gift packages by the country bus to my mother and enroll at Waltham College to do my Senior Cambridge. Mr. DaCosta offered me a contract to make picture frames for Tower Isle Hotel. This was a challenge to make about 150 frames with stock width of only half an inch wide, from Mahogany, Mahoe and Satin Wood. At the end of this contract I was asked to make a full set of household furniture for a friend who was getting married. This was the stepping stone for me to start my own furniture manufacturing, furniture retailing, haberdashery, and shoemaking.

Religion and Family

On May 8th. 1944 I accepted the Lord as my Savior and Master and this act was to direct the rest of my life. On June 8th, 1950 I married Daisy. This act too has greatly contributed to the direction of my life. By February 1954 we were blessed with three healthy boys. But, business wasn't going as well as expected. Although, I had moved the factory three times, I still had difficulty getting power for the three pieces of power tools I possessed and money was not always readily available to meet the needs of my now growing family. So I decided to immigrate to England; primarily to acquire more and better power tools.

My father gave me the fare to London, and I was advised by close friends to invest the money in the business rather than going to London, I chose to go to London because that was what I asked my father to assist me to do. I departed from Jamaica late April 1954 by air to New York and from there to England by a Dutch boat. I arrived in Southampton in early May.

Life In England

It was a cold day in early May when I arrived in South Hampton. A friend met me, and we then went to Way Bridge where my friend lived in a caravan. It was near the end World War II and we had to get a book of ration vouchers for each month. I got my first job to cut blocks for linoleum rolls. But it was difficult because the wood was stored outdoors in the cold wet weather and the band saw blades kept breaking. I left this job. I also left my old place and started sharing room with a friend that I met on the boat. He lived in Westford Park. I signed up at the Job Exchange (a job bank), and on the following Monday morning got a job in Hackney at a dining chair furniture manufacturing firm. This was very far, but I got a bicycle from a friend. I rode a bicycle to work from Great Western Road through Oxford Road, Oxford Circus, through Piccadilly and to Hackney. This was too far so I rented a room in Hackney which was so small that I could not turn around inside. If I wanted to turn around I had to go outside and then come back in. Also, I had to feed the meter for gas and electricity and there was just a night stand, a chair, and a bed. But it was okay since I could walk to work.

My wife came over in November of that year so I rented a bigger room in Studington. The problem was the room was in a cold attic—near to the roof. She got a job at the same firm where I worked. This was good as we worked together and walked to work together. Things got real difficult as my wife became pregnant with my 1st daughter. We moved from that house to one in Dalton. As soon as the landlord found she was pregnant he turned against us, and wanted us out of the room. The few Jews who rented rooms were skeptical, and locked the doors in the faces of blacks. English and Jewish children were scared of blacks—children would say "Mommy there goes a black man." The landlord at Hackney wanted us to move and so every Saturday morning he would sit at the dining table and after collecting his rent would politely say to me, "Victor I need the room." Things got very bad as the landlord started nagging my wife about moving out of his place. I remember one night I wept like a baby in the street after a Jewish woman locked the door in my face after I went to look at the room which she had advertised.

After sending home for children and mother, we joined a Pardner with a hand for £1 per week. The head of the Pardner was called the banker. She gave members the first and last draws and also borrowed money from others to assist us to buy houses. We bought a house in Edmonton on Arscott Road with our Pardner draw and by borrowing for everybody that we knew. This house was scheduled to be demolished for redevelopment. We moved in just before my first daughter was born in August of 1955—I think. This was challenging as the house had only 2 small bedrooms upstairs. Someone had taken the walls out of the dining and living, and there was no bathroom. But, we were accustomed to public baths—everybody went because very few houses had private bathrooms. In fact it was Jamaicans who let the English know that bathrooms could be placed inside of houses. To create more rooms we put back the partitions using old wood and cardboard boxes from dumps. Being a wood worker I did all of the work myself.

After our daughter was born we got a foster mother to keep her from Monday mornings to Friday evenings. We dropped our daughter off on a Monday morning and picked her up on Friday afternoons. To make ends meet we lived on very limited resources. We lived on scraggs of bacon. For the weekend meal we bought ½ head of pig for 2 shillings and 6 pence. On Sunday we stewed the tongue with broad beans and the rest was used to make stew peas to serve during the week and for lunch. There wasn't a fridge and so we preserved the food on the cold ledge outside. Sometimes we caught the trolley bus to Dalton, Intel and then to Hackney Empire—this worked well for sometime. More frequently we walked it up from Dalton to Edmonton to save every penny. To make the evening walk less boring we window shopped. We had to watch every penny.

We sent home money on a Saturday and it arrived in Jamaica on Tuesday. Three places Jamaicans went to each week—the post office for mail from Jamaica, the public bath and then shopping.

England was a university in and of itself for Jamaicans. Everyone learned to be self-sufficient and be on time. For example, once when the bus could not navigate the floods, we walked to work only to discover that we were late; every machine was working. We felt so ashamed. The workers were from the West Indies and had learnt this promptness from the English. If you told an Englishman "meet me at the bus park at 10:00 a.m. he will not be there at 9:58

a.m. or 10:03 a.m., he will be there at 10: a.m. sharp. The same things held true for church services people congregated on time and this Jamaicans learnt.

The English did everything for themselves even if they had money. This was unlike Jamaicans who if they had money would not do particular tasks. The boys came from Jamaica by daughter Angela's first birthday. My wife now had to stay home because we had a family of 4 children, and I had to look for a new job with greater income. A neighbor recommended the post office. When the furniture manufacturing firm at which I was working closed down for 2 weeks in August, I went and applied for a job at the post office. I got the post office job but was disappointed that my old factory job did not ask me to stay on as they normally did for other workers. On Friday evening when I asked to leave early at 4:00 p.m., rather then the usual 5:00 p.m., the boss took me into the office and told me he thought I was making the right move from industry to the civil service. He told me about his brother who became a fireman and was doing very well. I left the factory to become a postman doing collections and delivery in East Central London, Ludgate Hill, and the Bank of England areas. It was challenging having to work in winter and summer. After 2 years I took and passed the test for postman higher grade. I was promoted to the inland section. This job required much discipline and a lot of responsibilities, but it was difficult to work with the men as they called me Sunshine or Darkey. In a few months I graduated from my bicycle to a Quickly bike with the motor on the rear wheel. This was faster but provided no protection from the cold, and on arriving at work I could hardly stand from cold. I then bought my first Morris Traveler motor car about 18 months after the boys came from Jamaica. I joined the civil service motoring association and the family had fun driving over the place.

Life was still difficult economically as we had to watch every penny. At this stage I wanted to go back to Jamaica as initially I came to buy machinery and return after 3 years. Then my wife came and it turned into 5 years— eventually it was 10 years time and I thought it was time to do something about returning to Jamaica. I decided to enroll in Tottenham College (now the College of North East London) not to sit for exams but to keep abreast of trends in industry. I found though that for me to get along I had to sit exams. At the end of my 1st year I did my first exam, after the 2nd year I did intermediate and final. I continued and took another 2 exams—finally I did the full technician course. This was no fun—going to school and working from 10:00 a.m. to 7:00 p.m., and then to school by 9:00 a.m. In the winter I was hot as fire and sweated like a horse. I remember one lecturer said I should take a nap on the desk but felt embarrassed with the young students around.

Family life was good because my brother and I who lived in Birmingham were able to visit each alternately every other Christmas and this was very good.

Around this time I saw some lots of land advertised in the *Jamaica Gleaner* for £550. I paid down £5 and paid £5 every month. The 2 lots were in Washington Gardens. I paid quickly as I had to pay interest on the first lot. At first, I did not tell my wife that I had bought the second lot but did tell her after paying for the first. I did not pay interest on the second lot.

Going to school robbed me of the opportunity to work overtime. To earn more money I started selling mail order items to friends, but found that colored ladies did not have stocking which matched their clothing very well. So I dyed my own. I started with 6 dyed stockings and then moved on to producing them by the gross. Eventually I built my customers up to about 500 customers by visiting potential customers before going to work, and after work each day. On Saturday mornings around 8:00 a.m., I took all the children with me in the car. I had to put down the back seat and took along their potty. Most of the customers were in Stoudington, Tottenham, Dalton—I returned home by about 6:00 p.m. On Sundays after church I went to visit other customers in Hornsey Mosserel Hill. Besides stockings I sold other things like skirts, and blouses. I should take credit for introducing dark colored stockings for colored ladies and also for putting rhinestone on the stockings. It is amazing to see what has happened over the years, everybody is now selling dark colored stockings for ladies of different colors, not knowing how this started.

I changed my car every 2 years—my second car was a Triumph Companion. But those small cars did not have enough room for 6 children and 2 adults, so I bought a larger Volkswagen Caravan which was equipped with a double bed, 2 single beds, a little fridge and stove. I also bought a chemical toilet. By now the 3 boys were in the Boy Scouts movement and I also got a tent to go camping. Besides the civil service motoring association, I joined the caravan association club, did first aid at work and joined the St. John's Ambulance Brigade, did duty at football matches and rallies etc. We were always going out. We had rallies every bank holiday and in Easter had a camp lasting 3 days; life was very good. Because of my job I could take the children out whenever. Working at nights, I had many days off from the post office along with accrued sick time and annual leave, summer leave and winter leave.

Nothing succeeds like success. I had the best elementary education in Jamaica and the world. Those days science was integrated. I was very good at math. I was a bright student and got As in everything. Although I only passed 1st and 2nd year Jamaica Local Exam, I had a very good background. After 3, or 4 or 5 years of studying abroad I passed 2 final guilds exams, intermediate and full exams. Both included all of the parts. I did not expect to achieve this as I just went to school to keep abreast of technology. After passing exams I was surprised that I could get the certificates, I only got the pass slips. I was certified but not qualified, and had to prove that I:

1) Was over 25
2) Passed full sections of the exams.
3) Had industrial experience.
4) Fulfilled an apprenticeship
5) Passed intermediate exams
6) Passed a final exam.

I had pass slips for the exams, but thought I would not be able to provide the rest of documents since contracts tended to be informal rather than written. Also, by now it was now 12 years since I last worked in Jamaica. Nevertheless I took the bull by the horn and wrote a manager at one of my previous places of employment in Jamaica. To my surprise, he said just write and let me know what was wanted. I submitted this and earned my full technical certificate.

I was now at another cross roads—where do I go from here? I was informed that I could go into teaching by completing a compressed teacher educator course being offered for mature students—one could compress 4 years into 1 year. I applied and was accepted at Birmingham University, St Peter's College in Saltry. I decided to live on campus because studies lasted into the night be cause students had to do the full curriculum and this was intensive. How was I going to manage financially?" I got a student grant for £600, but this was not enough. There were other challenges such as living among young people who would not let me study. Man, at night, I could not do any work—younger students who had acquired the new disco lights would bang on my room door with invitations. Although we had a tutor to help assignments were challenging and some assignments had time consuming practicals. The greatest challenge was coming home because students were given assignments to be completed over 3 month long holidays. Students were not asked for assignments and would be automatically be failed if due dates were not met. The tutors would not be able to assist students if this failure occurred. Other challenges existed too as sometimes when I came home on the weekend I got comfortable with the family. If I did not catch the M1 on Mondays, I would miss 7:00 a.m. breakfast.

Money was definitely not enough and I decided to find some work. Average earning was £5 for men and £4 for women. Even the average English worker earned this also. One had to be really highly skilled to earn £1 more. I found a job in Hackney, in a factory making lolly, ice lolly. This job started at 6:00 a.m., and finished 6:00 p.m. The owner for the factory didn't ask your name because if he was caught he would say he didn't know you. On Friday he would just pay you in cash and that was the end of it. So it meant working 12 hours, and going home to work all night to complete the holiday assignments. This meant working all day and all night. When I went up to bed in the mornings my wife was just coming down. It meant working about twenty hours per day. I lost so much weight that I had to wear braces. I came down to about 135 lbs because I really lacked rest.

I graduated in December of 1969 from Sortly College, Birmingham University with a certificate in education. Now I was a teacher. I looked around for jobs, and all through the time I was in college I was looking at the advertisements in overseas *Gleaner* to see what was available in Jamaica. I applied, and got a lot of responses. One special one was from a joinery factory—I think it was for Arawak Woodwork. The lady called me in Birmingham like 3 or 4 times a week, wanting me to come home, but she would not meet the conditions I laid out. The conditions I laid out were (1) fair pay for my family, that is, my wife, myself and four children I was taking home to Jamaica; accommodations for 6 months while I constructed my home, for I had finished paying for one lot of land that I had. She wouldn't—she said well, I should pay my fare home, and then she would give me accommodations for like three months and if I proved satisfactory for the job then she would pay for the family. But I would not yield. I said I am not separating from my family, where one goes all go, all or nothing. Because I knew that I could do the job she wanted, I had no fear. So it was either that she had the faith in me or I wouldn't take the job; I didn't.

So I put that behind me. I got a job teaching at Crichton School in Moserel Hill. This was a challenging job because my first post, I was on probation for three months. But both staff and students were somewhat skeptical as I was the only black or colored teacher on the staff. His was a very big school. It had 2 wings, a north wing and a south wing I was in the south wing. The staff generally was quite nice, quite friendly. One or two weren't very nice and the headmaster, Mr. Lowes was a real gentleman, and the department head, Mr. Spackman, he too was good. The only real adversary I had was the gentleman who was senior in my department he taught technical drawing as myself. But eventually when I put him in his place he was quiet, I had no more problem. It was good, I was a 3rd form teacher, and the kids were fantastic. We had to do assembly once a month and when my turn came, it was sort of difficult getting them to do what I wanted them to do. I was a 3-3-1 the top class and they were so appreciative of where I brought them to that when they became 4-3-1 they came to me just the same and said, "Sir aren't you proud of your 3-3-1 how we are good". They were very good now, they were bright coming forward doing assembly although I had to coax them into it and bring them, they appreciate the fact that they had matured enough that they didn't have to be prompted and bribed to come on.

Being a form teacher in England was different from being one in Jamaica. In England the children were like your own and the parents too treated you like family. Whatever anything went wrong with any of the children they would come to you. It wasn't rare that on a night the telephone would ring at 11:00 or 12:00 a.m. It would be a mother calling and say, "Sir, Mr. Victor, Johnny hasn't come home or I'm having problem with Mary or so." It was real good. Many a lunch time, I didn't have time for lunch as I was busy counseling students. Although the school provided subsidized lunch, and it was very cheap, I don't remember the figure now, but at times I had to pay for 2, 3, 4 lunches because the children just didn't have any lunch money, but it was real fun. My hobby was flower arrangement, and I sent my students into the bushes to collect branches, and I also placed quizzes from the overseas newspaper on the classroom door for students to complete.

Another event was good there, every month the 4th and 5th form students had chaperoned house parties. It was not like Jamaica with eating and dancing. Instead it was a real fellowship with people eating, and they sat on the floor, talking—it was a comradely kind of a thing.

While at Crichton I was really intent on coming home and kept looking at newspaper advertisements. Eventually I saw that they were recruiting teachers. I applied, attended the interview and was successful.

In Jamaica

I was selected to teach at Jamaica College in Jamaica on a contract. The Jamaican government paid the fares of my family and all I needed was somewhere to live. But I was also intent on going back into furniture making. When I came to Jamaica in 1966 I saw a sale sign—I called the agent to secure the property for me after seeing it from the outside, and gave the realtor permission to sell one of my lots in Washington Gardens.

My wife did not want me to return to woodwork, but I still crated a box of machinery and sent them home. While I was driving the nails in the crate she was down on me. Coming home I resigned from Crichton School during the July, school holiday.

I asked the government to book our passage via New York. The idea was to spend time in New York and to give my furniture and machinery time to arrive by ship at the same time when I arrived in Jamaica. It was a very sad and pleasant day at my church when they had a send off farewell for us It was a small Church with a membership of about 80 and every family was represented at that send-off. People broke their vacation just to be there on that Saturday afternoon. It was really moving because the Englishman loves his holiday. He will not break his holiday for anything and they all came. They all could not understand why I wanted to go back home. I was happy from having a good job and a 4 bedroom council house. Everything was fine, I was in the St. John's Ambulance I was a member of the whole community but yet they wished me Godspeed and that was it. We flew from Heathrow to New York and we spent time with my wife's sister-in-law. It was a trying week. It was extremely hot but we survived.

When we got home, we had a dear friend, who was more than a father who received the goods that came by sea, he had made a shed for the machinery and secured them at the shop that I had bought. We spent the first 4 weeks,or so at his home then got a cottage supposedly on rent— the owners had a big door factory in Kingston, and I decided to help them in my free time, as they did not have the technical knowledge to run the factory. It was good, although I did not know what was going to happen later on because trying to get somewhere to rent was very difficult. But after about a month or two they thought we were going to stay there forever. Although some members of the family were kind to us, like their sister, and two brothers, there was one brother that wasn't pleasant at all. He kept harassing us, "when you going to get out." He kept harassing us so much that the children became edgy. When I came home in the evenings they asked, "Daddy, when are we going to find somewhere?" We would jump in the car and drive all over trying to find somewhere. I couldn't get anywhere to rent with the family. Eventually, we saw houses in Edgewater selling and we decided we would try to get one. Unfortunately, when my wife went to look at the house, my wife said she did not want to live in any matches box, and that was the end of it. I took back the money from the people and so we were back at square one. When I told this to the real estate gentleman that got the place for me, he said to me, "boy don't you do that, why did you take back your money from the lady for the house? Ask her to get you another one, don't even phone her go and talk with her, and when you get it just take your children and put there because if the wife don't want to come well at least your children will have shelter." I did that, and went down and saw the lady. Well, all the houses were sold out and none were available. I had to wait until someone had defaulted on meeting the requirements for their mortgage. Well she called me after about 3 or 4 weeks, said she got one and I should go and look at it. I said don't bother just get it for me. I left Jamaica College when I got the call I went straight down to her office, but in filling up the form although I found that although I was getting marriage allowance, housing allowance and was department head— my salary was not enough to get a mortgage of about JA$12,000. Luckily I was working at the furniture business and the owners wrote a letter stating that I was earning extra money. When we moved in the children were very excited. It took about 3 months to get electricity and at nights we went collecting tiles, there were no fences between neighbors. That was very good. Then we turned attention to cleaning-up the shop—that was when we got a rude awakening. The last China man who rented the shop dumped his refuse at the back, and there were mounds of pigeon droppings, broken windows. The four children and myself cleaned up the shop but this was difficult and took many months. One thing we did—we brought home a little Morris or Austin 1100CC from England which I bought at a junk yard. I fixed it up like a new car and once a month we filled it up with gas, which cost about 30 cents per gallon, and went either to the beach or touring around the island. When I got my diary I marked off a day when we went all over the island. We continued what we started in England. Both jobs in England gave me time with the family.

I could not set up a furniture factory for the first few years as we were cleaning up the place and putting everything back in good condition. We hired one good man who was a mason, the factory took a few months to build and then we put in the machines. My first customer, Vaz Prep, bought 100 chairs and wanted them in a few weeks. I had a real production line as the combination machinery we brought from England could saw thickets, cut tenons, make mortises, sharpened its own blades. The factory was now up and running. I now had to get someone one to run the factory. We got a lady in about 1974 or so. She was able to manage the factory while I worked at Jamaica College (JC). Working at JC was another challenge because they had a woodwork department—but no technical drawing. They had an unskilled technical drawing teacher who left after the first term. I was left on my own to teach wood work, metal work and technical drawing

At JC I found to my dismay that the administration gave me a 3rd form again. I kept wondering why they gave me a 3rd form again. Added to this I was also a house master for Hardy House which was a first year house and this was great challenge. I was subject teacher, house master and form teacher.

At the end of the year, at vacation time I not only had to make reports for the student I taught, I also signed as a form teacher and as a house master. But I managed due to good time management.

The first year was not bad but by the 3rd year I sent the first class up for exams. I can remember being the only teacher to prepare 2 classes containing 40 students simultaneously for O'levels. The first year pass rate was not too good, but it was still good. The following rate was quite good.

My contract with the government was for 2 years. By the third renewal of my 2 year contract I decided to take my family back to London. Naturally their fares were already paid back to London. I kept looking for a better job, and filled out an application at the Bureau of Standards. Meanwhile the boys in England were doing well. I had gotten them a Council house. This was not common but because we were upstanding member of the community the rules were bent. The one condition that they laid down was that my sons had to have a father figure. A friend of mine took this challenge, and he had to sign a paper. I also I created a 2 signature approving joint account. It made sense to leave the boys there because they were ready for University. The disappointment was that they did not return after completing school.

While in England the Jamaica Bureau of Standard offered me the opportunity to set up a furniture department. All of the positions I got were great challenges. All I got was a chair and a desk. I had to get staff, equipment for the laboratory. For about a year I sat at my desk mapping out things.

While at the Bureau of standard I had a supermarket and made furniture for school and for Courts (a large British furniture company). He retired from this and went back on contract and consultant work starting factories in different Caribbean islands. I retired from this last job.

Reg's Story: Illustrating Mid-Colonial Capital Returnees

In 1932 I was born in a little district called Lodgie Green in Clarendon, but the main Grantham post office where births and deaths were registered was used as the identifying address. My mother was a housewife, and my father was a farmer of yams, banana, sugar cane, and he also reared cattle.

At the time land was rented from the "big backras". These backras were the white property owners. We had two backras named Sutton and Percy Junior and then the government of Jamaica bought the lands and turned it into settlements. The government did this because renting land from backras did not provide security for the settlers. On rented lands one could not plant long term crops like coconuts or build permanent concrete homes.

My mother had 3 children before marrying my step-father, and their union produced 5 children: 3 girls and 2 boys. After marrying she took me to live with her new husband since I was the last. The other 2 brothers remained with their father. My father was a good man.

Before going to England in 1961, life was very tough economically in Jamaica. At the time there was a market for all farm produce. Milk was sold to a condensery, and ground food was sold to the entrepreneurs who after buying the produce from us transported it to Kingston from the nearby train station in Frankfield. Banana was shipped, and the sugar cane was sold to a local factory. The income was regular as the condensery paid us for the milk every fortnight. But it was not enough to acquire the life I have now. As poor people, we were happy with our provision of daily food from the farm. Our main concern was to have money to pay the doctor's bill, and clothes in preparation for an accident. If there were an accident, necessitating medical care, neighbors would take it as their responsibility to ask for the doctor's money, and the hospital clothes. If the money was loaned out, the borrower would repay it quickly.

I went to Grantham Kilsyth Elementary School at 7 years old. Before going to school I did not think about differences among people, but on going to school I observed immediately that light skinned children were treated better than dark skinned children. I later saw this in my town where the Chinese, white and brown children were treated differently. My mother's relatives were light skinned although she was a dark skinned Maroon. As a result of my light skinned relatives, even though I am dark skinned, I did not suffer as much ill treatment as other dark skinned children who had no fair skinned relatives. This sense of protection convinced me that forging relationships with those of a fairer hue (though without compromising my sense of cultural identity) would serve to improve my quality of life. I vowed from age 7 that the woman I marry would be fair skinned as I considered that such a union would give my children an improved quality of life. And at age 14 I predicted that I would get married at the age of 26. I judged that by this age I would have acquired enough resources from farming to be a man capable of caring for a family.

My elementary school had different grades starting with A, then B, junior class and then 1st class upward to 6th standard. At the end of elementary school one could do an additional 2 years to prepare for taking 1st, 2nd and 3rd year Jamaica Local Exams. Sixth standard prepared students for farming, manual labor jobs, and being a police officer, or a pupil teacher. First and 2nd year Local Exams prepared students for entry level careers, like being an assistant postal clerk. Third year Local Exams prepared students for fully fledged upper level positions in careers such being a post mistress.

At that time the only way to make money as a black boy was to farm or take up a trade. I stopped at 6th standard because I could not afford the cost of books and education. The year 1951 was a turning point in my life as I left school and went into farming hoping that would take me to the end. I combined my 6th standard qualification, which was a fairly good education, along with the practical experience gained from seeing my father tending to the cattle and entered farming. But, I noticed that one could not make enough money from farming. This was most evident after the 1951 hurricane which flattened every crop, and drowned animals. As a farmer I was left standing just like Alice in Wonderland with nothing. The hurricane was the first devastating blow to me as young farmer. I noticed that the only people making money were those with a trade.

I then decided to pick up cabinet making at age 19 in my cousin's shop. This shop was in Grantham—it was an ordinary room in a 2 story board shop. My cousin's furniture manufacturing shop occupied one room on the lower floor. He was the main furniture maker in town who brought a wealth of knowledge about making furniture from having worked in Kingston (the capital city of Jamaica) to rural Grantham.

I can remember the transition from being a farmer to a worker dressed up in khaki uniform with shined boots. Once at work I was under my cousin's control. It was like an army as on arriving at work, every morning my cousin inspected my appearance for visible seams in my shirt's arms and my pants. He looked me up and down as he sat facing the front door while appearing to be reading his newspaper. Although workers were not paid for dressing-up; it was part of the discipline. This is a discipline that young people today lack.

There was another boy who worked for my cousin, but I had preference because I was the owner's cousin and a member of an extended family that had high color and status. My job duties were to first sweep out the store and then learn woodwork by pushing a wood plane and using the manual saw to cut wood accurately. Developing the art of sawing was a slow process which helped furniture makers to avoid becoming tired. Although it makes sense now, back then I felt that my cousin did not push me ahead and that he did not want me to make furniture too quickly. But I had an urge to move forward quickly and in my first week made a picture frame from scrap timber. I remember the first time I made a bookcase and my cousin's surprise at my accomplishment. He asked in surprise, "When did you learn how to make furniture?" But all the time I was watching him.

This apprenticeship to my cousin lasted for about 1 year because the shop was too much of a confinement after having grown up on a farm. Also while learning woodwork I was paying workers to do work on my farm and I was supporting myself from the farm proceeds (my cousin did not pay me much; if anything.

It was about 1956 when I left and went into building construction with Mr. Jus Francis who was known to train many boys at the time. The system in Jamaica was an English styled apprenticeship where one worked with a local authority or a skilled professional for a time and then moved on to create one's own business. Back then most buildings were made of wood. Later cement blocks came into vogue. I brought my accuracy in using a saw, plane and chisel from making furniture to constructing buildings. The first day of work Mr. Francis paid me, and this was unusual. He saw that I could do his work very well. One memorable house is still standing today that I helped to construct back then. To get to work I walked to a place called Riches from Lodgie Green to arrive at work by 8:00 a.m., and put out the necessary tools for other workmen. These skills from furniture making and building construction are what I used to make life.

Each week I received 2 shillings and 6 pence from Mr. Francis. This income along with income from my farm meant that I was like a big shot with plenty of money, and I was partially an employer, which was one of my ambitions. Life was good, as when the construction trade was slow I sold oranges, sugar cane, cows, and pigs. I was among the elite as I bought my first bicycle and built a 2 room concrete house on the one acre of land I bought from the government through my father. This was not uncommon, as parents made sure that their children gained settlement. Because of my dexterity I also built my own furniture for my home.

I fulfilled my childhood prediction and got married at age 26 to my wife who came from Mandeville but grew up in my district with her aunt. It was not very common among my peers to buy land, marry and rise from humble economic circumstances. I planned my family, how many children, and how far away from home I should take jobs. I was now the local builder. My first child was born in 1959. I had a second child this was part of our plan.

I did not want to leave Jamaica, but all of my elementary school books called Caribbean Readers were about England, my cousin who had migrated encouraged me, and this was where others were going to seek for fortune and fame; but I always said no. Even my cousin with whom I learned furniture building was already in England.

Then, one day after coming home from the farm, I went for walk and while looking at the beauty of my field after the rain I decided to go. I came home, told my wife about my decision, the next morning I went to the travel agency and later in March of 1961 left for London; she joined me in February of 1962. My wife had enough money to keep her for 3 months. I traveled on just an official sheet of paper because the island was out of passports. Later we received British passports because after August 1962 Jamaica gained independence and that was when the Jamaican passport started.

In England

I arrived by ship at Southampton dock and then caught a train to Victoria Station, London. I then took a taxi home to my uncle where I lived for 6 months. We shared a room and bills. It was the tradition to stay with family members until one became financially stable.

In the following days after arriving in England I signed up with the Exchange for employment and received my first job as a carpenter joiner with the local Council authority. I made £12 per week.

On the first job I did not pay attention to racism. But, I saw racism in housing and the job advertisements which told blacks to not apply. I avoided confrontation with the English, but they provoked blacks by the way they talked to you. If sent to do a job you could not refuse like white workers did. If black employees voiced their dislike for a task then they would have to leave that job.

My first room was rented from a man on my job. One day I said to him, "Do you know where there is a room for rent?" He said, "Are you serious?" I said, "yes." All of this time he was noticing me and that afternoon took me home, turned his living room into a bedroom and rented this room to me. The house was a big house on Nicoll Road in Harlesden, North West London. The house was fully carpeted, had a fridge, and a modern bathroom. There were other tenants but I lived with the family on the 2nd floor, while their daughters who were married lived below.

In 1962 my wife joined me in London—she settled our two children with their grand-parents, and the land and house which we owned were left in the care of my brothers and father. In London my wife worked full-time in a factory making lamps and after that for a short period as a 3rd shift nursing assistant.

She left nursing because the night shift was too taxing. Her weekly wage was only £5, and out of this sum she sent some to care for those children who were left with our parents in Jamaica, paid our living expenses in England, government National Insurance, and saved. Sometimes I wonder how we did so much with so little. When I think about all of the hardships, nobody in Jamaica should grudge us for what we have.

My first job ended after 2 years because the Council's building project finished and the council jobs were now being outsourced to private contractors. My second job as a structural carpenter was with Wimpy, one of the biggest construction companies in England. This job was welcomed growth as my pay increased to between £18 to £25 per week and I was now doing priced work per job. I was in line for more money as a good worker, but I did not seek for promotion which did not increase my pay.

On my second job the working conditions improved as I was now assimilated into English culture and understood slang words. I was also going to Willesden Technical College where I learned to sketch frames, and then build them. I spent 2 years there. Two major constructions I was a part of were the Center Point building in London, and the London Bridge Project.

Going to church was my major recreation. I was comfortable in my church and also went to Bible College. My knowledge of church was so much that I could help others to interpret the Bible. When I went to bible school it helped me to learn how to interact with others who suffered problems at work and at home. I was always like a counselor.

I was a settled family man and started to think about owning my own apartment with my own key. I bought my first 2 storey, 3 bedroom house on Yewfield Road in the Willesden area of London from my savings. I lived in Willesden from 1964 until 1972. It was a mixed neighborhood and we were the 2nd black family to move there—not many came after. We were the only black family on the whole block. I did not have to do anything special to save money to purchase this house because from the day I left school I was industrious and refused to stay where I was financially. I bought my first car in the mid 1960s too—it was a Riley Woolsey. It was a joy to pick up my wife from work and drive to work. This was an improved living.

When homes were bought, the friendships formed in one rooms broke because some bought homes outside of London—in different cities and in the country parts, where we felt more accepted by whites and other blacks. Now, the only time we saw old friends was when we visited each other on special occasions. But owning our homes provided more rooms for later Jamaican migrants as the owners lived in a small section of the house and rented out the rest of rooms. Bathrooms and kitchens were shared.

When possible, West Indians maintained friendships by attending each others birthday parties, etc. Jamaicans were the leading group among West Indian migrants. My third child was born in England, 1963, followed by two more children. I left those children who were born in Jamaica because they represented my roots and culture—unfortunately they are both deceased. This was one reason I took those of my children who were born in England to Jamaica so that they would grow together.

My 3rd job was as a carpenter with a subcontractor. It was rare for me to stay in one company. I never experienced racism personally, only signs of racism from the jobs that some whites got. I suspected that they got the meaty part of the job and someone like me did the odds and ends. Some blacks made a fuss but I did not. After all someone has to do the odds and ends of any job and I was getting my money.

We did not have any outright personal racist experiences in England, but were denied work and housing. I remember having to live in one bedroom apartments because English people would not permit blacks to live in their houses. Sometimes rooms were advertised but when we showed up the owners said they were already rented. But when whites went they were able to rent these same rooms. To get rooms Jamaicans asked whites friends to sublet rooms and then blacks sneaked in at night. Those Jamaicans who went up in the early 1950s were lucky enough to rent rooms in dilapidated buildings that were slated to be torn down. These lucky Jamaicans then sublet to others. Sometimes there were six people in one room taking turns to sleep. Some slept in the day and went to work at night and those who worked at night slept in the day.

Since blacks were excluded from social activities, these rooms served for our private social activities, dining room, living room and bedroom. After work we bought liquor and food, and visited each other's room. We would sit and talk, play cards and as Jamaicans all over we loved loud music, but the landlord would call the police. This was one example of how living in England forced changes in Jamaican habits.

On Sundays these same rooms were used for church. This is how the Pentecostal Church movement and the returned residents association we have since taken back to Jamaica, was started in England; out of Jamaican immigrants who were not accepted by the white church and in one rooms. On Sundays when others came for church, if there were not enough chairs then visitors brought their own chairs.

As people had more children they moved into Council flats which had 2-3 rooms and private bathrooms/kitchen and then into semi- or fully detached houses. These houses back then could cost as little as £4,000. We helped each other to save the down payment for buying homes by throwing Pardner.

At age 26 I planned to return to Jamaica within 10 years mainly to establish myself in my field of endeavor. Money was not available to vacation with a young family—too expensive. I said if I remained in Jamaica I would have been rich.

Another reason for planning to return was I realized that blacks did not get the best of anything, and I became worried over my children after going to their school and observing that black children could do as they wanted. I remember the revealing conversations that took place at an end of term open day. One teacher asked my wife, "What is your child like at home?" White people are like that they are not real smart, but they play on what others say. My wife said my daughter was head strong. The teacher said, "I noticed that she comes in some days and does not want to do any work, and then on another day she will." The teacher said that when my daughter did not want to work she lets her do as she wanted.

I said to my wife, "we are going home." I put the house on the market and it was sold in a few days. The furniture was stored for a month and then shipped to Jamaica. In the meantime after the house was sold, we lived with a friend for that month.

In Jamaica I moved in with my wife's parents who were happy to have us. On arriving in Jamaica in 1972 I settled my children in Kilsyth Primary School, in Grantham. This was back to my roots. I also lined out my house in Kilsyth but one afternoon just changed my mind. Then my brother came to me and said

"Mr. Freckleton said, if you want land he can sell you a lot in Spaldings." I wrote a check immediately without seeing the lot—the owner of the land was so happy for the money that he thought that my check was full payment for the lot but I said no, that it was just a deposit.

My wife asked me how I was going to manage in Jamaica without work, but, if I could not find someone to take care of them I made up my mind to remain. Luckily I was able to board my children with relatives in Sanguinetti then in Spaldings and they attended Spalding Primary School, and then Knox High School. They returned to England in 1978 and today these children are doing well—my daughter is a Solicitor, my first son is a manager with a local government authority and my youngest son is a systems analyst. They all say thanks for sending them back as this gave them the foundation to succeed.

After 13 months in Jamaica my children were fully settled in school and I went back to England. I realized that my passport was gold because my friends wished for the opportunities I had in England and here I was sitting on a passport. That wasn't right as I could use this passport to help my friends to survive. I went back to England and stayed with a friend and then with my cousin. I went back to my 3rd job in England as a subcontractor. This second tenure lasted for 2 years until I joined Bovis (one of the largest construction companies in England) as a carpenter. I remained with Bovis until about 2 years before I returned to Jamaica in 1997. I was active in church and British politics—that is of course my children's country. The difficulty was to bring my children up in a British culture while maintaining my own. I was a trade unionist (highly active and respected in the field of industrial relations) and this meant being involved in local politics. I was the main union negotiator representing the interests of some 800 workers' health and safety working conditions. I was also involved in these people's social issues—any domestic problems they were faced with that affected their work they would share with me. I was the proverbial "Agony Aunt"—a person who resolves problems like a counselor. The recession came in the early 1990s and Bovis lost work. This galvanized my efforts in another direction—I subcontracted on my own and formed my own refurbishing construction company which got off to a promising start. Just as I was about to expand the business, taking on larger building contracts and running simultaneous crews, the last two projects in England took me under. I was unable to deliver on these property projects I had been commissioned to undertake, because my doctor advised me to quit working or face the possibility of dying due to stress and physical exhaustion. I did not know that people could be so difficult because the projects were 80% complete but the owners would not accept them or give me back the money that I had invested. I vowed never to build another property again.

I came home to Jamaica for the second and final time in 1997, but my wife came in 1999 because she was still on the work force earning her pension. In the early years she worked full time and could afford to make the necessary NIS contributions to earn a full pension. But, when more children came along she could only work part time and this lowered her pension contributions. In the final 13 years she worked with the local government helping elderly people. This full time job provided the needed funds to make up for the previous short fall in NIS contributions, so that she could get a full government pension in 1999. During my time with Bovis I sent money home and my house was already built from 1973 to provide boarding accommodation for the nearby high school and community college students.

What changed in Jamaica from the time I came home in 1972 to 1998? Politics and violence has changed. I recall in 1976 there was a state of emergency in Jamaica. But there is always a welcome for Reg because I came home often. The longest I stayed away after going back to England was 2 years. I can be identified by accent but it has been to my advantage.

What are some positives aspects of returning home? Positives are what I can do and that is accepted by others. Boarding students is a positive and it is a life long dream come true from 12 years of planning. Boarding creates an immediate family – the children see me as Dad, and I have more money than I need. I rent out one side of my house to boarders from the local high school and community college. This provides a good income for me and my wife which is complemented by our pension from England. I have used my house as a refuge to the community and for students who cannot pay. Many times I give free boarding to students who cannot afford it. This makes me feel like I am making a contribution. It is possible that without such help a young person might have dropped out of school.

Another positive is being able to farm, to produce food instead of having to buy. Boarding and farming have made me an employer and also another means of giving back to the local community.

The church is a major part of my life where God, through me, performs healing and I live out the word of God. I formed a growing Pentecostal church in Alston. We had zinc shed at first but now we are leveling the land for a more permanent structure.

Negatives: Some boarders spoil it for others and (their parents) do not pay and leave owing up to JA$25,000, and people are not always grateful for the contributions I have made.

People are not always trustworthy and like to spite returnees. For example, I went into farming but could not get access to any markets because people blocked me as a returnee. The people that I depended on did not help me. In one case I rented a piece of land where the owner also planted. He promised to get me an order but twice he made excuses. I went at an odd time and found him digging yams for this same buyer.

I left this first rented land and went to Lodgie Green among my nephews and brothers and like the first experience, they only helped when I spent money to plant. When they needed markets they got it, and sold their stuff when I was not around. Because I could not do the reaping each time I walked away and all the money invested went down the drain. I get respect but no support at the point when I am looking for returns, it is as if they pull the carpet. I then went to farm in Ballieston near to where I have the church. Members now support my farming venture by preparing the land, planting the crops and finding the markets. I don't look at negatives I move on, whatever I set out to do nothing stops me.

Farming is what I know, and that is the contribution I can make. This is not feasible in carpentry. For example, I put in a letter to the principal at the community college to do free carpenter's labor. The letter was passed on to the head of the staff. I was supposed to do 2 half day's as a contribution but the head staff claimed I was coming to take away jobs.

Farming does not have these restrictions as I give away food and people are grateful. It is interesting how things have come full circle in my returning to farming in Jamaica—my roots. Another negative is thieves. This is the biggest problem in Jamaica. To tackle this obstacle, I hardly let anyone past my

front porch and that goes for certain relatives too. In many crimes against return residents, it is their own re-
latives or people they know that set up other people to come and rob them. For example, in England I lived side by side with a returnee who went to live in St Elizabeth and her brother and his son cut her throat because they said she was too mean.

Hardly any relatives come into my home to scrutinize it and assess what I have. I have one house cleaner and there are certain parts of the house she does not go. If a relative comes to visit I take them to this porch. England is not my home. Jamaica is, I am at home but don't expose myself to undue situations.

Life among Jamaicans can become monotonous and that is one purpose of belonging to a returned residents association where I can meet those who know my experiences and can hold a conversation about other problems than money. I was introduced to the returned residents associations through my boarding/dorm house mother—she was the secretary. The president was teacher at her school. I joined in 1997. Membership cost JA$800. The association provides friendships with some migrants that I knew before leaving Jamaica and some friendships I have constructed. For example, I knew the current president of my returned resident's association before leaving Jamaica and she delivered my children in England. In returning residents associations there is a common understanding between us. After having been away from Jamaica for 40 years we have lost friendships. Since it takes a while to redevelop friendships this association serves as central meeting place.

One of my biggest concerns is to get the young people who are in England involved in what we have started. If they don't then all of our work here will die. Our children are unlikely to return to reside permanently here in Jamaica. As professionals in England, my children command good competitive salaries which cannot be matched in Jamaica. They do not consider themselves Jamaican neither are they English in the Anglo-Saxon sense of the word. My children consider themselves to be British citizens who are of Jamaican parentage. Nevertheless, I live in hope that they will not abandon their culturally rich and diverse Jamaican heritage

I have lived what others have written in books about racism and how Britain has changed. It's Jamaicans who made Britain what it is. When Jamaicans went to England, English people did not even own their own houses, but they stared to after we started to buy houses and fix them up. English people use to bath in their kitchen sink, had little or no inside bathrooms, and left bread unwrapped until we went and showed them the necessity of wrapping bread in paper and taking a daily bath. We made Britain what it is today. When I was buying houses, my bank manger told me to just let him know how much I needed, because I was never late with a payment, and I would repay all my loans by selling one house to buy another. The banks' money was just to close the deal on the new house until the old one sold.

Luckily, I started preparing to come home from 1972, when I built this house in Jamaica. I took time off, came to Jamaica and built it myself since I was already a building contractor.

To regain entry I have moved back near to my community. I am of the opinion that it is not only Jamaicans who think that returned residents are strangers but returned residents make themselves into strangers. I try to get along by living among the people. When I go in the market I run a little joke with the traders and I say, "here is some more give it to your friend too." If I am buying groceries I buy extra for somebody else in the community and I often give money and groceries to the needy. Some Jamaicans, however, are not to be trusted and have concluded that if I loan someone money I should not expect repayment.

I recognize that there are limits to my success. Although I received the British Empire medal from the Queen in 1987 for my contribution to the building industry and to the Union of Construction, Allied Trades and Technicians (UCATT) (Britain's only specialist construction workers union) and contribution to my NW London community and with that, I have certain privileges, including to St Paul's Cathedral, London, which permits baptisms and marriages at the Cathedral for 3 generations (my two grand-children were baptized there), I still feel that if I were fairer skinned my life would have been better, perhaps less of a struggle than it was. This is not to detract from my achievements of which I am very proud, though I have to say that when you look around you see evidence of this. My wife was told in England that she was different because she as a brown person and so was able to provide better care for her patients. Here in my town businesses have shut down yet the only store to survive is owned by a fair skinned Jamaican. If you go down to the two hardware stores, the one owned by the black person is a different store than the store owned by the mulatto. I realize that I am respected for my money but the mulatto store owner would not invite me home for dinner.

Returnees are said to be labeled with the 3 Ms: they are mad, they are mean and they have money. I told one store owner, if I lay down and let you walk over me, then you'll say I am a good man. But if I complain then you say I am mad. One has to be diplomatic as it seems that all Jamaicans want is money!

BIBLIOGRAPHY

Adams, Jr., R. H. 1998. "Remittances, Investment, and Rural Asset Accumulation in Pakistan." *Economic Development and Cultural Change*, 47(1):155-73.

Adler, Patricia. 1985. *Wheeling and Dealing: An Ethnography of An Upper-Level Drug Dealing*. New York: University Press.

Allette, Brenda A. 1994. *My Double Life*. New York: Carlton Press.

Alvarez, Hernandez. 1967. *Return Migration to Puerto Rico*. Berkeley: Institute of International Studies, University of California.

Amin, S. 1974. "Modern Migrations in Western Africa." *Modern Migrations in Western Africa*. London: Oxford University Press.

Anwar, M. 1979. *The Myth of Return: Pakistanis in Britain*. London: Heinemann.

Associated Press, October 2003.

Atkinson, Robert. 1998. *The Life Story Interview*. London: Sage.

Bailey, Benjamin. 2002. *Language Race and Negotiation of Identity*. New York: LFB Publishing LLC.

Bailey, Carol. 1996. *A Guide to Field Research*. Thousand Oaks, California: Pine Forge Press.

Bandon, Alexander. 1994. *West Indian Americans*. New York: Maxwell McMillan.

Becker, Howard S. 1998. *Tricks of the Trade: How to Think About Your Research While You're Doing It*. Chicago: The University of Chicago Press.

Becker, Howard S. 1953. "Becoming a Marijuana User." *American Journal of Sociology* 59:235-42.

Bennett, Natalie. D. 2002. Work Makes A Woman? Gender, *Ethnicity, and Work In Afro-Caribbean Immigrant Women's Lives*. Unpublished Ph.D. Dissertation: University of Michigan.

Berg, E. J. 1961. "Backward-Sloping Labor Supply Functions in Dual Economies - The Africa Case." *Quarterly Journal of Economics*. 75:468-566.

Bernard, Headley, Michael Gordon and Andrew Macintosh. 2005. *Deported Volume 1*. Kingston, Jamaica: Bible Society of Jamaica.

Blumer, Herbert. 1969. *Symbolic Interaction: Perspective and Method*. Englewood Cliffs, N.J.: Prentice-Hall.

Bodnar, John. 1985. *The Transplanted: History of Immigrants in Urban America.* Bloo-
mington Indiana: Indiana University Press.
Booth, Heather. 1992. *Migration Process in Britain and West Germany.* Vermont: Ash-
gate Publishing.
Booth, Alan, Ann C. Crouter and Nancy Landale (eds.). 1997. *Immigration and the
Family.* New Jersey: Lawrence Erlbaum Associates Publishers.
Borgas, George. 1985. "Assimilation, Changes in Cohort Quality and the Earnings of
Immigrants." *Journal of Labor Economics.* 3:463-89.
Bovenkerk, F. 1974. *The Sociology of Return Migration: A Bibliographic Essay.* Hague:
Nijhoff.
Boyd, Nancy (ed). 2001. *Culturally Diverse Parent-child and Family Relationships: A
Guide for Social Workers and Other Practitioners.* New York: Columbia University
Press.
Brookes, D. 1969. "Who Will Go Back." *Race Today.* September 132-4.
Brooks, D. 1975. *Race and Labor in London Transport.* London, England: Oxford Uni-
versity Press.
Byerless, D. 1974 "Rural-Urban Migration in Africa: Theory, Policy and Research Impli-
cations." *International Migration Review,* 8:543-66.
Byron, Margaret and Stephanie Condon. 1996. "A Comparative Study of Caribbean Re-
turn Migration From Britain and France: Towards a Context - Dependent Explana-
tion." *Transactions of the Institute of British Geography* Vol. 21, Number 1, March
1996.
Cajoleas, L.P. 1959. "The American-Educated Foreign Student Returns Home." In
Teachers College Record 60 (4):19-197.
Caldiera, Teresa. 2000. *City of Walls: Crime, Crime, Segregation, and Citizenship in São
Paulo.* Berkley, California: University of California Press.
Calliste, Agnes. 1983. "Women of Exceptional Merit: Immigration of Caribbean Nurses
to Canada." *Canadian Journal of Women and the Law.* 6:85-102.
Carter Center. 1998. *The Observation of the 1997 Jamaican Elections.* Atlanta: Carter
Center. 15-50.
Cassarino, Jean-Pierre. 2004. "Theorizing Return Migration: The Conceptual Approach
to Return Migrants Revisited." *International Journal on Multicultural Societies.*
2004, 6,(2) 253-79.
Castles, Stephen and Mark Miller. 1993. *The Age of Migration.* New York: The Guilford
Press.
Cerase, F. P. 1974. "Migration and Social Change: Expectations and Reality. A Study of
Return Migration from the United States to Italy." *International Migration Review* 8
(2) 245-62.
————1970. "Nostalgia or Disenchantment: Considerations on Return Migration."
The Italian Experience in the United States. New York: Center for Migration Stu-
dies.
Chamberlin, Mary. 1997. Narratives of Exile and Return. New York: St. Martin's Press.
Chaney, Elsa. 1985. *From Neighbor to Stranger: Dilemma of Caribbean People in the
US.* New Haven, CT: Yale University Press.
Charmaz, K. 1990. "Discovering Chronic Illness: Using Grounded Theory." *Social
Science and Medicine.* 30, 11, 1161-72.
Clarke, Velta J. 1994. *Aliens in a New Frontier: Caribbean Immigration into the United
States and the Interchanging of Human Resources, Opportunities in Education.*
Brooklyn, NY: Caribbean Research Center Medgar Evers College, CUNY.
Clarke, Velta J., and Emmanuel Riviere, eds. (1989) *Establishing New Lives: Selected
Readings on Caribbean Immigrants in New York City.* Brooklyn, NY: Caribbean

Research Center, Medgar Evers College, CUNY.

Connel, J. B. Dasgupta, R. Laishley, and M. Lipton. 1976. "Migration from Rural Areas: The Evidence." *Village Studies*. New Delhi: Oxford University Press.

Corbin, J. 1986. "Qualitative Data Analysis for Grounded Theory." In *From Practice to Grounded Theory: Qualitative Research in Nursing*. Edited by W. C. Chenitz, J.M. Swanson. Menlo Park: Addison-Wesley.

Cornelius, W. A. 1991. "Labor Migration to the United States: Development Outcomes and Alternatives in Mexican Sending Communities." In *Region and Sectoral Developments in Mexico as Alternatives to Migration*, edited by S. Diaz-Briquets and S. Weintraub. Boulder: Westview Press, Inc.

Cornelius, W. A. and P. L. Martin.1993. *The Uncertain Connection: Free Trade and Mexico-US. Migration*. San Diego, CA: Center for U.S.-Mexican Studies.

Cornell, Stephen, Douglas Hartmann. 1998. *Ethnicity and Race: Making Identities in a Changing World*. London, England: Pine Forge Press

Crawford-Brown, Claudette and J. Melrose Rattery. 2001. *Parent-Child Relationships in Caribbean Families. Culturally Diverse Parent-Child and Family Relationships*. New York, NY: Columbia University Press.

Daley, Vernon. *Jamaica Gleaner*, December 9, 1999.

Dasgupta, B. 1981. "Rural-Urban Migration and Rural Development." *Why People Move*. Paris, France. UNESCO.

David, T.1976. *Prisoners Among US: The Problem of Parole*. Washington D.C.: Brookings Institute.

DaVanzo, J. 1981. "Microeconomic Approaches to Studying Migration Decisions." In *Migration Decision Making: Multidisciplinary Approaches to Micro-level Studies in Developed and Developing Countries, edited by* G.E De Jong and R.W Gardner: New York: Pergamon.

Davison, R B. 1962. "No Place Back Home: A Study of Jamaicans Returning To Kingston, Jamaica." *Race* 9 (4): 499-509.

Denzin, Norman.K 1989a. *The Research Act: A Theoretical Introduction to Sociological Methods*. Englewood Cliffs, CA: Prentice Hall.

——————.1989b *Interpretive Interactionism*. Newbury Park, CA: Sage Publications.

Dickson, David. 1995. *Memoirs of An Isolate*. Ormando Beach, Florida: Corporate Image Publishing Company.

Dominguez, Virginia. 1975. *From Neighbor to Stranger: The Dilemma of Caribbean Peoples in the United States*. New Haven, CT.: Antilles Research Program, Yale University.

Douglas, Lisa. 1992. *The Power of Sentiment: Love, Hierarchy, and the Jamaican Family Elite*. Boulder, CO: Westview Press.

Dumon. W. 1979. "The Situation of Children of Migrants and Their Adaptation and Integration in the Host Society." *International Migration*. 17(1/2):59-75.

Durand, J., E. Parrado and D. Massey. 1996. "International Migration and Development in Mexican Communities." *Demography* 33 (2): 249-64.

Durand, J. and D. S. Massey.1992. "Mexican Migration to the United States: A Critical Review." *Latin American Research Review*. 27(2): 3-42.

Eppink. A. 1979. "Social Psychological Problems of Migrant Children and Cultural Conflicts." *International Migration*. 17 (1/2): 87-119.

Erickson, Rosemary; Waymen J. Crow; Louis A. Zurcher, and Archie Connett. 1973. *Paroled But Not Free*. New York, NY. Behavior Publications.

Farley, Reynolds and Walter Allen. 1987. *The Color Line and the Quality of Life in America*. New York, NY: Russell Sage Foundation.

Ferguson, Ira Lunan. 1967. *I Dug Graves by Night to Attend College by Day: An Autobiography.* Brooklyn, NY: T. Gaus's Sons.

Filstead, William ED. 1972. *Qualitative Methodology: Firsthand Involvement with the Social World.* Chicago, IL: Markham Publishing Company.

Fitzpatrick, Joseph. 1971. *Puerto Rican Americans: The Meaning of Migration in the Mainland.* Englewood, CA: Prentice Hall.

Forner, Nancy. 1987. *New Immigrants in New York.* New York. NY: Columbia University Press.

————1978. *Jamaica Farewell: Jamaican Migrants in London.* Berkley, CA: University of California Press.

Foner, Nancy, Rubén G. Rumbaut and Steven J. Gold. 2000. *Immigration Research for a New Century: Multidisciplinary Perspectives.* New York, NY: Russell Sage Foundation.

Fortney, J. A. 1970. "The International Migration of Professionals." *Population Studies* 12 (2):217-32.

Gans, Herbert J. 1997. "Toward a Reconciliation of "Assimilation" and "Pluralism": The Interplay of Acculturation and Ethnic Retention." *International Migration Review,* 31 (4), 875-92.

————1992. "Second Generation Decline: Scenarios for the Economic and Ethnic Features of the Post-1965 American Immigrants." *Ethnic and Racial Studies* 15 (2) 173-92.

Giddens, Anthony. 1991. *Modernity and Self-Identity.* Stanford CA: Stanford University Press.

Gilroy, Paul. 1993. *The Black Atlantic: Modernity and Double Consciousness.* Cambridge MA: Harvard University Press.

————1987. "There Ain't No Black In the Union Jack." *The Culture Politics of Race and Nation.* London, England: Unwin Hyman.

Gladwell, Joyce. 1969 [2001]. *Brown Face, Big Master.* New York, NY: Doctor Bird Press.

Gladwell, Malcom. 1996. "Black Like Them." *The New Yorker:* April 29 and May 6, 1996:74-81.

Glaser, B. 1978. *Theoretical Sensitivity.* Mill Valley, Sociology Press.

Glaser,B and A. Strauss. 1967. *The Discovery of Grounded Theory.* New York, NY: Aldine.

Glaser, A. 1978. *The Brain Drain: Emigration and Return.* Oxford, England: Pergamon.

Glass, R. 1960. *Newcomers.* London, England: Center for Urban Studies.

Glazer, Nathan and Daniel Patrick Moynihan. 1965. *Beyond the Melting Pot: The Negroes, Puerto Ricans, Jews, Italians, and Irish in New York City.* Cambridge, MA: The MIT Press.

Glick-Schiller, Nina and Georges Fouron. 2001. *Georges Woke Up Laughing: Long Distance Nationalism and Searches for Home.* Durham, NC: Duke University Press.

Glick-Schiller, Nina, Linda Basch, and Cristina Szanton-Blanc. 1992. *Towards a Transnational Perspective on Migration: Race, Class, Ethnicity, and Nationalism Reconsidered.* New York, NY: New York Academy of Sciences.

Globerman. Steven. (ed.). 1992. *The Immigration Dilemma.* Vancouver, Canada: The Frasier Institute.

Gmelch, G. 1992. *Double Passage: The Lives of Caribbean Migrants Abroad and Back Home.* Ann Arbor, MI: University of Michigan Press.

Gmelch, G. 1980. "Return Migration." *Annual Review of Anthropology* 9: 135-59

Goffman, Ervin. 1959a. *Stigma: Notes on the Management of Spoiled Identity.* Englewood. CA: Prentice Hall.

Golden, Patricia. M. (ed.). 1976. *The Research Experience*. Itasca, IL: F. E Peacocks Publishers Inc.

Goldstein, S. 1978. "Circulation in the Context of Total Mobility in S.E. Asia." *Papers of the East West Population Institute*. No.53, August.

Gordon, Monica. 1979. *Identification and Adaptation: A Study of Two Groups of Jamaican Immigrants in New York City*. Ph.D. Dissertation, City University of New York.

Gunst, Laurie. 1995. *Born Fi Dead: A Journey Through The Jamaican Posse Underworld*. New York, NY: H. Holt.

Goulbourne, Harry. 1999. "Exodus?: Some Social and Policy Implications of Return Migration from the UK to the Commonwealth Caribbean in the 1990s." *Policy Studies*. 20 (4) 157-72.

Hardin, Garrett. 1973. *The Immigration Dilemma: Avoiding the Tragedy of the Commons*. : Washington, DC: Federation for American Immigration Reform.

Harris, C. 1987. "British Capitalism, Migration and Relative Surplus Population: Synopsis." In *Migration* 1 (1) 47-90.

Harris, J. R. and M. P. Todaro. 1970. "Migration, Unemployment, and Development: Two-sector Analysis." *American Economic Review* 60:126-142.

Henke, Holger. 2001. *The New Americans: The West Indian Americans*. Westport, CT: Greenwood Press.

Hickling, Frederick W. 1991. "Double Jeopardy: Psychopathology of Black Mentally Ill Returned Migrants To Jamaica." *International Journal of Social Psychiatry* 37 (2): 80-89.

Hinds, D. 1966. *Journey to an Illusion*. London, England: Heinneman.

Hill, J. K. 1987 "Immigrant Decisions Concerning Duration of Stay and Migratory Frequency." *Journal of Development Economics* 25:221-34.

Hintzen, Percy C. 2001. *West Indians in the West: Self Representations in an Immigrant Community*. New York, NY: New York University Press.

Hollinger, David. 1995. *Postethnic America: Beyond Multiculturalism*. New York, NY: Basic Books.

Ho, Christine. 1999. "Caribbean Transnationalism as a Gendered Process." *Latin American Perspective* 26(5): 34-54.

Horney, Karen. 1937. *The Neurotic Personality of our Time*. London, England: Kegan Paul.

Jamaica Gleaner. June 22, 2005.

Jamaica Gleaner. August 9, 2004.

Jamaica Gleaner. June 11, 2004.

Jamaica Gleaner. November 12, 2003.

Jamaica Gleaner. October 23, 2003.

Jamaica Gleaner. August 8, 2003.

Jamaican Criminal Justice Research Unit. 2000. *Deportee Study Executive Summary*. Unpublished.

James, Winston. 1992. "Migration, Racism and Identity: The Caribbean Experience in Britain." *New Left Movement* 193:15-56

Johnson, Violet. 2005. "Culture, Economic Stability, and Entrepreneurship: The Case of British West Indians in Boston." In *New Migrants in the Marketplace* edited by Marilyn Halter. Amherst, MA: The University Press.

Kalmijn Matthijs. 1996 "The Socioeconomic Assimilation of Caribbean American Blacks." In *Social Forces* 74 (3): 911-30.

Keats, D. 1969. *Back In Asia*. Canberra, Australia: Australia National University.

Kessner, Thomas and Betty Caroli. 1982. *Today's Immigrants: Their Stories*. New York, NY: Oxford University Press.

King, Russell, Alan Strachan and Jill Mortimer. 1983. "Return Migration a Review of The Literature." *Geography* 19.

Kizilbash, M. 1964. "The Employment of Return US Educated Indians." *Comparative Education Review* 8 (3): 320-326.

Koch, C.W. 1977. "Jamaican Blacks and their Descendants in Costa Rica." *Social and Economic Studies* 26 (3): 339-361.

Kosack, G. 1976. "Migrant Women: The Move to Western Europe—A Step Towards Emancipation?" *Race and Class* 17 (4) 369-379.

Kuper, Adam. 1976. *Changing Jamaica*. London, England: Routledge and Kegan Paul.

Laporte, Bryce. 1990. *Emerging Perspectives of the Black Diaspora*. London, England: University Press of America.

Lee, E. S. 1966. "A Theory of Migration." *Demography* 3(1):47-57.

Levitt, Peggy. 2001. *The Transnational Villager*. Berkeley, CA: University of California Press.

————2000. "Migrants Participate Across Borders: Towards an Understanding of Its Forms and Consequences." In *Immigration Research for a New Century: Multidisciplinary Perspectives,* edited by Nancy Foner, Rubén G. Rumbaut and Steven J. Gold. New York, NY: Russell Sage Foundation.

Light, Ivan and Steven Gold. 2000. *Ethnic Economies*. New York, NY: Academic Press.

Lin, Nan, Ronald S. Burt and John Vaughn. 1976. *Conducting Social Research*. New York, NY: McGraw-Hill Book Company.

Lindstrom, D. P. 1996. "Economic Opportunity in Mexico and Return Migration from the United States." *Demography* 33(3): 357-374.

Lipton. M. 1980. "Migration from Rural Areas of Poor Countries: The Impact on Rural Productivity and Income Distribution." *World Development* 8 (1): 1-24.

Lowenthal, David and Lambros Comitas (eds.). 1973. *Consequences of Class and Color: West Indian Perspectives*. New York, NY: Anchor Press.

Lyons, Beverly, P. 1950. *Sociocultural Differences Between American-born and West Indian-born Elderly Blacks: A Comparative Study of Health and Social Service Use*. New York, NY: Garland Publishers.

Mahler, Sarah. 1995. *America Dreaming: Immigrant Life on the Margins*. Princeton, NJ: Princeton University Press.

Mahler, Sarah and Patricia.Pessar. 2001. "Genderized Geographies of Power: Analyzing Gender Across Transnational Spaces." *Identities* 7 (4): 441-459.

Mains, Susan. P. 2000. *Mobility and Exclusion: Toward an Understanding of Migration in the Context of Jamaica*. Unpublished Paper.

Massey, D. Borgatta.1990. "The Social and Economic Origins of Immigration." *Annals of the American Academy of Political and Social Science* 510: 60-72.

Massey, D. Borgatta. 1986. "The Social Organization of Mexican Migration to the United States." *Annals of the American Academy of Political and Social Science* 487:102-13.

Massey, D. S., J. Durand and H. Gonzalez.1987. *Return to Aztlan: The Social Process of International Migration from Western Mexico*. Berkeley, CA: University of California Press.

Massey, D. S. and K. E. Espinosa. 1997. "What's Driving Mexico-U.S. Migration? A Theoretical, Empirical, and Policy Analysis." *American Journal of Sociology* 102 (4):939-99.

Massey, D. S. and F. Garcia Espafia. 1987. "The Social Process of International Migration." *Science* 237: 733-38.

Massey, D. S. and F. Garcia Espafia. 1994. "An Evaluation of International Migration Theory: The North American Case." *Population and Development Review* 20:699-

751.

Massey, D. S. and F Garcia Espafia. 1993. "Theories of International Migration: A Review and Appraisal." *Population and Development Review* 19:431-66.

Menjiver, Cecelia. 2000. *Fragmented Ties: Salvadorian Immigrant Networks in America.* Berkley CA: University of California Press.

Mincer, J. 1987. "Family Migration Decisions." *Journal of Political Economy* 86 (5):749-73.

Moore, Joan W.1970. "International Colonialism: The Case of The Mexican Americans." *Social Problems* 17:463-71

Moser, Caroline and Holland, Jeremy. 1997. *Urban Poverty and Violence in Jamaica .* Washington, D.C.: World Bank February 1997: 2, 13-15.

Moynihan, D.P. 1965. *The Negro Family: The Case for National Action.* U.S. Department of Labor.

Murphy. R. 2002. *How Migration Labor is Changing Rural China.* Cambridge, MA: Cambridge University Press.

National Committee on Political Tribalism. *Report of the National Committee on Political Tribalism* (Kingston, Jamaica: Government   of Jamaica, 23 July 1997):11-13,29,53.

Nelson, J.M. 1976. "Sojourners Versus New Urbanites: Causes and Consequences of Temporary Versus Permanent Cityward Migration in Developing Countries." *Economic Development and Cultural Change* 24(4):721-757.

Nettleford, Rex. 1978. *Caribbean Cultural Identity: The Case of Jamaica.* UCLA Latin American Center Publications, University of California. Los Angles, CA.

Newton, V. 1984. *The Silver Men: West Indian Labor Migration to Panama, 1850-1914.* Institute of Social and Economic Research: University of the West Indies.

Noguera, Pedro. "Exporting the Undesirable: An Analysis of the Factors Influencing the Deportation of Immigrants from the United States and an Examination of their Impact on Caribbean and Central American Societies." *Wadabagei.* 2 (1).

Olwig, Karen Fog. 1993. *Global Culture Island Identity: Continuity and Change in the Afro-Caribbean Community of Nevis.* Philadelphia, PA: Harwood Academic Publishers.

Patterson, Orlamdo. 1968. "West Indian Migrants Returning Home: Some Observations" *Race* 10 (1): 69-77.

————1963. *Dark Strangers: A Study of West Indians in London.* London, England: Tavistock.

Palmer, Ransford. 1995. *Pilgrims from the Sun: West Indian Migration to America.* New York, NY: Twayne Publishers.

Park, Robert E. 1928. "Human Migration and Marginal Man." *American Journal of Sociology* 33:881-93.

Payne, Douglas W. 1998. *The 1997 Jamaica Elections: Post-Section Report.* Washington D.C.: Center for Strategic and International Studies, 21 January 1998: 9-10.

Pessar, Patricia (ed.). 1997. *Caribbean Circuits: New Directions in the Study of Caribbean Migration.* Center for Migration Studies: New York, NY.

Phillips, Mike and Trevor Phillips. 1998. *Windrush: The Irresistible Rise of Multi-Racial Britian.* London, England: Harper Collins Publishers.

Philpott. S. B. 1977. "The Monserratians: Migration Dependency and the Maintenance of Island Ties in England: Between Two Cultures." Oxford, England: Blackwell.

————1973. *West Indian Migration: The Montserrat Case.* London, England: Atlone Press.

————1969. "Remittance Obligations, Social Networks and Choice Among Monserra tian Migrants in Britain." *Man* 3 (3): 465-67.

Portes, Alejandro and Min Zhou. 1993 "The New Second Generation: Segmented Assimilation and Its Variants." *Annals of the American Academy of Political and Social Science* 530:74-96.

Poston, Dudly. 1994. "Patterns of Economic Attainment of Foreign Born Male Workers in the US." *International Migration Review* 28(3): 78-500.

Prescod-Roberts, Margaret. 1980. *Black Women: Bringing it all Back Home.* Bristol, England: Falling Wall Press.

Prus, Robert. 1996. *Symbolic Interaction and Ethnographic Research: Intersubjectivity and the Study of Human Lived Experience.* Albany, NY: State University of New York Press.

Ravenstein, E.G. 1989. "The Laws of Migration II." *Journal of Royal Statistical Society* 52 (2):1241-305.

————1985. "The Laws of Migration I." *Journal of Royal Statistical Society* 48 (2):167-235.

Reiff, Tana. 1993. *Never So Good: The Jamaicans.* Belmont, CA: Feron/Janus.

Richard, Randall. 2003. "Exporting Crime: US Send Criminal Aliens Home." *The State*, Section D, October 26, 2003.

Richardson, Bonham C. 1983. *Caribbean Migrants: Environment and Human Survival on St. Kitts and Nevis.* Knoxville, TN: University of Tennessee Press.

Robotham, Don. 2000. "Blackening The Jamaican Nation: The Travails of A Black Bourgeoisie in A Globalized World." *Identities* 1070289x, March Vol 7, Issue 1.

————1998. "Transnationalism in the Caribbean." *American Ethnologis* 25 (2): 307-21.

Rodriguez, Nestor. 1987. "Undocumented Central Americans in Houston: Diverse Populations." *International Migration Review* 21 (1): 4-26.

Rosenberg, Matthew. "Jamaican Leader Vows to Stop Gangs." *Associated Press.* Kingston, Jamaica: 12 July 1999.

Rubenstein. H. 1979. "The Return Ideology in West Indian Migration." *Papers in Anthropology* 20 (1): 21-38.

Saloutos, T. 1956. *They Remember America: The Story of the Repatriated Greek-Americans.* Berkeley, CA: University of California Press.

Sarup, Madan. 1996. *Identity Culture and the Postmodern World.* Edinburgh, England: Edinburgh University Press.

Shibutani, Tamotsu and Kian M. Kwan. 1965. *Ethnic Stratification.* New York, NY: The MacMillan Company.

Shover, Neal. 1985. *Aging Criminals.* Beverly Hills, CA: Sage Publications.

Simey, T.S. 1946. *Welfare and Planning in the West Indies.* Oxford, England: Clarendon Press.

Sjaastad, L. A. 1962. "The Costs and Returns of Human Migration." *Journal of Political Economy* 70(Supplement): 80-93.

Snow, David. 1993. *Down on Their Luck: A Study of Homeless Street People.* Berkley, CA: University of California Press.

Sobo, Elisa Janie. 1993. *One Blood: The Jamaican Body.* State University Press of New York: Albany, NY.

Somers, Margaret and Gloria Gibson. 1994. "Reclaiming the Epistemological "Other": Narrative and the Social Constitution of Identity." *Social Theory and Politics of Identity.* (Ed.) by Craig Calhoun. Cambridge, MA: Blackwell.

Sotnequist, Everett V. 1937. *The Marginal Man: Study in Personality and Culture Conflict.* New York, NY: Charles Scribner's Sons.

Sowell, Thomas. 1981. *Ethnic America: A History.* New York, NY: Basic Books.

Speckmann, Lamur H.E. and John D. Speckman (eds.). 1975. *Adaptation of Immigrants from the Caribbean in the European and American Metropolis.* Department of Anthropology and Non-Western Sociology, University of Amsterdam: Leiden.

Spradley, James. 1979. *The Ethnographic Interview.* New York, NY: Holt, Rinehart and Watson.

Stark, 0. 1991. *The Migration of Labor.* Cambridge, MA: Basil Blackwell.

Stinner, William, Klaus De Albuquerque and Roy Bryce Laporte (eds.) 1982. *Return Migration and Remittances: Developing a Caribbean Perspective.* Washington DC: Smithsonian Institute.

Stone, Carl. 1991. "Race and Economic Power in Jamaica." In *Garvey: His Work and Impact.* Edited by Rupert Lewis and Patrick Bryan. Trenton, NY: African World Press.

Taylor, Dorceta E. 1992. *Identity in Ethnic Leisure Pursuits.* San Francisco, CA: Mellen Research University Press.

Taylor, Edward. 1976. "The Social Adjustment of Returned Migrants to Jamaica." *In Ethnicity in America.* Edited by Frances Henry, pp 213-230. The Hagure: Mouton.

Taylor, J. E. 1999. "The New Economics of Labour Migration and the Role of Remittances in the Migration Process." *International Migration* 37 (l):63-88.

————1987. "Undocumented Mexico-U.S. Migration and the Returns to Households in Rural Mexico." *American Journal of Agricultural Economics,* 69:626-38.

Thomas, B. 1973. *Migration and Economic Growth: A Study of Great Britain and the Atlantic Economy.* Cambridge, MA: Cambridge University Press.

Thomas, W.I. and Florian Znaniecki. 1927. *The Polish Peasant in Europe and America.* Boston, MA: R.G. Badger.

Thomas-Hope, Elizabeth. 1999. "Return Migration to Jamaica and its Development Potential." *International Migration* 37 (1): 183-207.

————1988. "Caribbean Skilled International Migration and the Transnational Household." *Geoforum* 19 (4): 423-32.

————1986. "Transients and Settlers: Varieties of Caribbean Migrants and the Socio-Economic Implications of their Return." *International Migration.* Geneva 24 (3): 559-71.

Todaro, M. P. 1969. "A Model of Labor Migration and Urban Unemployment in Less Developed Countries." *American Economic Review* 59 (l):138-48.

Townsend, Fred D. 1991. *Farming to Glory: A Jamaican Family Chronicle.* Shippensburg, PA: Companion Press.

Ueda, Reed. 1994. *Postwar Immigrant America.* Boston, MA: Bedford Books of St. Martins Press.

Useem, J. and R.H. Useem. 1955. *The Western Educated Man in India.* New York, NY: Dryden Press.

U.S. Immigration and Naturalization Service. 2001. *Statistical Yearbook of the Immigration and Naturalization Service.* U.S. Washington, DC: Government Printing Office.

Vickerman, Milton. 1999. *Crosscurrents: West Indian Immigrants and Race.* New York, NY: Oxford University Press.

Vulliamy, E. "Roots of Violence." *The New Republic* 22 (7): 13-14.

Waldinger, Roger. 2007. "The Bounded Community : Turning Foreigners into Americans in 21st Century Los Angeles." *Ethnic and Racial Studies* 30 (7) 341-74.

————1996. *Still the Promised City: African-Americans and New Immigrants in Post industrial New York.* Cambridge, MA: Harvard University Press.

Wallerstein, I. 1974. *The Modern World System I. Capitalist Agriculture and the Origins of the Modern World Economy in the Sixteenth Century.* New York, NY: Academic Press.

Waters, Mary C. 1999. *Black Identities: West Indian Immigrant Dreams and American Realities*: Cambridge, MA: Harvard University Press.

————1994. "Ethnic and Racial Identities of Second Generation Black Immigrants in New York City." *International Migration Review* 29:515-44.

————1990. *Ethnic Options: Choosing Identities in America*. Berkley, CA: University of California Press.

Waters, Mary C. et al. 2002. "Transnationalism and the Children of Immigrants in Contemporary New York." In *The Changing Face of Home: The Transnational Lives of the Second Generation*. Edited by Mary Waters and Peggy Levitt. New York, NY: Russell Sage Foundation Press.

Wheeler, Stanton. "Socialization in Correctional Communities." *American Sociological Review* 26:697-791.

Wiest. R.E. 1979. "Anthropology Perspectives on Return Migration: a Critical Commentary." *Papers in Anthropology* 20 (1):167-87.

World Bank. *Violence and Urban Poverty in Jamaica: Breaking the Cycle*. Washington D.C.: World Bank, 31 January 1997: 7 ,40,42.

Zelinsky, Wilbur. 1971. "The Hypothesis of the Mobility Transition." *Geographical Review* 61 (2): 219-49.

INDEX

ABOUT THE AUTHOR

Alex Miller was born in Jamaica, West Indies when the popularity of migrating to England waned, and Jamaicans began to take greater interest in gaining socio-economic mobility in America. He provides an insider's perspective, having lived the immigrant experience while earning a Ph.D. in Sociology, a Master of Arts in Sociology (both from the University of South Carolina); and a Master of Divinity (Erskine, 1998). He also holds a Bachelors of Arts (University of The West Indies, 1986). Over the past six years he has taught sociology and courses in religion at various colleges and universities in South Carolina, USA. As a budding scholar, he is committed to theoretical thinking, and as a first generation immigrant, to slowly deepening sociological understandings about migration phenomena that have been esoteric—as exemplified in this work.

REVIEW

Alex Miller's Migration Can Fall Apart: Life Stories from Voluntary and Deportee Return Migrants is an insightful extension of contemporary studies of return migration. The book is also a pleasure to read in that much of the story is literally told by return migrants in their own colorful, and sometimes painfully truthful, styles. The subjects of the study are migrants returning to Jamaica after living in the UK or the US. The main scholarly contribution of the work is in the way it considers how three key elements of return migration result in a sorting out process that leaves many returnees disappointed in their reception. These elements are the concept of colonial capital, deportees as part of the return migrant stream, and transnational identity. By helping the reader understand the importance of colonial capital in Jamaican culture, and by applying this concept to an analysis of voluntary and non-voluntary (deportees) return migrants, Miller explicates how it comes about that returnees who vary widely in their achievements abroad, and who vary in their Jamaican social origins, may face rejection by countrymen. Miller concludes that only a minority of return migrants can accurately be described as truly transnational migrants. With this finding he cautions against an overly zealous attribution of transnational explanations in the study of return migration.

Dr. Jimy Sanders
Graduate Director
University of South Carolina
Columbia Campus

ENDORSEMENT

Comprehending the varying complexities of migration—both internal and external—of the people of the English-speaking Caribbean has for years challenged the region's scholars. Leaving home for the promise of better economic opportunities abroad began for Jamaicans in the period following Emancipation, as hope diminished for the country's cane-cutter slave descendants for a better life in an emancipated Jamaica. The pattern only increased in the years leading up to and following Independence, when "going foreign" began including sizeable numbers of the island's middle classes. An excellent contribution that this worthwhile volume makes to further sociological understanding of the many sides of Jamaican out-migration is the author's use of the term "colonial capital." Miller's methodological analysis of how acquisition of "colonial capital"—by which he means migrants' capacity to successfully negotiate the world's metro poles—gives insightful understanding of key attendant elements within Caribbean and Jamaican migration; important among them are development of trans-nationalism, deportation, and return migration. I recommend the book as a useful supplement for courses in the history and sociology of the Caribbean.

Bernard Headley
Professor of Criminology
University of the West Indies, Mona
Author of *Deported* (2005)

www.ingramcontent.com/pod-product-compliance
Lightning Source LLC
Chambersburg PA
CBHW050717280326
41926CB00088B/3111